Right-Minded Teamwork in Any Team

The Ultimate Team Building Method to
Create a Team That Works as One

Do No Harm.
Work As One.®

By
Dan Hogan
Certified Master Facilitator

Books by Dan Hogan

Reason, Ego, & the Right-Minded Teamwork Myth*: The Philosophy and Process for Creating a Right-Minded Team That Works Together as One*

Right-Minded Teamwork in Any Team*: The Ultimate Team Building Method to Create a Team That Works as One*

How to Facilitate Team Work Agreements*: A Practical, 10-Step Process for Building a Right-Minded Team That Works as One*

How to Apply the Right Choice Model*:*
Create a Right-Minded Team That Works as One

7 Mindfulness Training Lessons*: Improve Teammates' Ability to Work as One with Right-Minded Thinking*

Right-Minded Teamwork*:*
9 Right Choices for Building a Team That Works as One

Design a Right-Minded, Team-Building Workshop*:*
12 Steps to Create a Team That Works as One

Achieve Your Organization's Strategic Plan*: Create a Right-Minded Team Management System to Ensure All Teams Work as One*

Contact Dan Hogan at Dan.Hogan@RightMindedTeamwork.com

ISBN: 978-1-939585-05-9

Acknowledgments & Appreciations

To the thousands of teammates, team leaders,
and team-building facilitators with whom I've
worked with over the last 40 years,

Thank You

For being my teacher.

Collectively, we created this
awesome team-building program.

*Right-Minded Teamwork is a business-oriented,
psychological approach to team building where
acceptance, forgiveness, and adjustment
are teammate characteristics,
and customer satisfaction
is the team's result.*

In addition, there are several special people I want to joyfully acknowledge and thank for their contributions.

First and foremost, I want to convey my deep and heartfelt gratitude to our editor, Erin Leigh. Thanks to her superb editing and vital guidance, Right-Minded Teamwork is now much easier to understand and successfully integrate in your team. Thank you, Erin. The RMT book series would not have happened without you.
(To contact Erin, email erin@thechoice.life.)

Next, a giant thank you to the Ebook Launch team. Dane Low, our book cover designer, created exceptional cover designs for the Right-Minded Teamwork book series. Thank you for elevating Right-Minded Teamwork. (To reach Dane visit EbookLaunch.com.)

Another sincere thank you goes out to Cathi Bosco, our graphic artist, who renovated and modernized many of our Right-Minded Teamwork process models, graphics, and illustrations
(reach her at CathiBosco.com).
And I also want to thank the Media A-Team, who created the original and current versions of the Right Choice Model
(find them at Mediaateam.com).

Finally, I want to express my gratitude to Jackie D'Elia, our website and UX designer, who successfully modernized the RightMindedTeamwork.com website into an easy-to-use platform. Her work allows us to share the RMT books, models, and other resources and materials with the world. Thank you, Jackie.
(Contact Jackie at JackieDElia.com.)

CONTENTS

5
Elements of
Right-Minded
TEAMWORK

Psychological Goals
Achieve Emotionally-Intelligent
Teammate
Work Behavior
2
3
Work
Agreements
Create and Follow
Commitments
Business
Goals
Achieve 100% Team
Customer Satisfaction
1
Framework:
2 Goals
+
3 Methods
=
100% Team Customer
Satisfaction
Let's go!
Apply the Three
Workshop Implementation
Plan to incorporate
all 5 Elements
4
Operating
System
Build an Effective &
Efficient
Operating System
5
Teammate
Strengthen
Individual Performance
6 - 12 Month Continuous Improvement Plan

Preface

Welcome to Right-Minded Teamwork ® (RMT).

What is RMT?

Right-Minded Teamwork is an intelligent and empowering teamwork system that creates a *team that works together as one*.

It is everyone's right to work together as *one unified team*, and every person may exercise their right – right now if they choose. That is why RMT is for everyone, everywhere, forever, and it is available to you right now.

Dear Reader, apply RMT and you will improve your work processes and strengthen your relationships.

Apply RMT, and your team will achieve 100% customer satisfaction.

Apply RMT, and your team will *work together as one.*

You'll also do your part to make the world a better place for everyone, everywhere, forever. Let's get started right now.

It is an honor to introduce you to this unique, real-world, continuous improvement method. RMT has already improved the lives and teams of thousands of people worldwide. Apply this process in your team, and you, too, will reap its benefits.

Before we get started, you may be wondering if you're in the right place. Is this book for you? What should you expect to learn? Why is this methodology worth considering? Let's go ahead and answer these questions right now.

Is this book for you?

This book is primarily intended as a resource for leaders and facilitators. But it is also much more than that. The content you will find here can positively benefit everyone, everywhere, on any team.

What is this book about?

Right-Minded Teamwork is practical. It is a universal, self-evident, self-validating process.

RMT produces positive business results by allowing your team to work together as one and get real work done. RMT naturally motivates teammates to grow.

In these pages, you will learn about RMT's 5 Element framework and how to apply RMT in your team. Once you understand each Element, you will understand how Right-Minded Teamwork will directly benefit your team and your team's customers.

In summary,

> *Right-Minded Teamwork is a business-oriented, psychological approach to team building where acceptance, forgiveness, and adjustment are teammate characteristics, and 100% customer satisfaction is the team's result.*

How does RMT produce real-world benefits?

There are many common “team building” practices out there. Three common team-building avenues include education, games, and social events.

As far as real team building goes, none of these approaches is effective. Not one of them produces proven, reliable results. If you have participated in them, you know what I mean.

Still, many well-meaning team leaders continue to use these ineffective tactics, trying to make them work. Usually, this is because they do not realize *there is a better way.*

Real-World Team Building

A **real-world approach** to team building ***is the better way***. It is also the most reliable way to achieve and sustain high-performance teamwork.

Right-Minded Teamwork ***is*** a real-world, team-building process.

Applied intentionally, it has the power to transform your team, bring you together to work as one, and allow you to achieve or even exceed your goals. This kind of result is why real-world team building is most certainly worthy of your serious consideration.

Where did RMT come from?

This proven methodology came from people just like you.

Over the course of my 40-year career in team building and facilitation, I had the honor of working with hundreds of teams and thousands of beautifully diverse people all around the world. As much as I was hired to help them, they also taught me, every time.

Together, we uncovered the core methods and process of Right-Minded Teamwork. Our collective wisdom revealed them.

I also like to believe these methods are universal and have been available to all of us since the beginning of time.

Over the years, I strived to capture, distill, and teach these RMT concepts and practices, refining the model over time. Today, it is as clear as it has ever been - and easier than ever for you to understand and apply the RMT framework with your team.

As I often said to those beautiful people over the last 40 years, *"You were my teacher. Collectively, we created this team-building program, a process we eventually named Right-Minded Teamwork."*

Now you get to reap the rewards, too.

What makes RMT unique?

In my entire team-building career, I've never seen another real-world, team-building process like RMT. (And I've looked, I promise).

There are a few practices out there that hold some similarities. They are terrific processes, and they can be helpful in certain circumstances. They can be excellent tools to have in your toolbox. But these practices are built to stand alone, not to function as an integral part of your team.

Right-Minded Teamwork is intended to be applied within your team to support you and grow with you.

To clarify RMT's uniqueness, think for a moment about what you really want for your team. I'm guessing it includes:

- a proven, reliable, easy-to-follow approach to continuous improvement
- a way to consistently resolve real issues to sustain high-performance teamwork

No, I'm not reading your mind. I've simply worked with a lot of conscientious leaders and facilitators who, like you, wanted the best for their teams and weren't quite sure how to get there.

With RMT, you will undoubtedly achieve both goals.

The RMT process will show you how to resolve team issues in a safe, compassionate, and caring way (referred to as "a **moment of Reason**" or a "Right-Minded thought system"). RMT tools like **Work Agreements**, the **Right Choice Model**, and the **7 Mindfulness Training Lessons** will improve your team's relationships as well as your work processes, giving you everything your team needs to come together and work as one.

When you integrate RMT's framework and tools into your team, you ensure your team has the ability to hear and address - not avoid! - those crucial conversations that must happen to recover from challenging situations and achieve team goals.

How does RMT address team issues?

What happens when you and your teammates address your issues in a Right-Minded Teamwork way?

Here is what you will do. When difficult team situations occur, you and your teammates consistently **accept**, **forgive**, and **adjust** your collective attitudes and behaviors. This real-time adjustment allows you to successfully respond and recover from those challenging situations. By resolving the underlying problems, you pave the way for productive teamwork.

Doing so is not always easy, but it really is that simple.

In the following pages, I will introduce you to ***Work Agreements***, the ***Right Choice Model,*** and the ***7 Mindfulness Training Lessons*** that explore Right-Minded Teamwork Thinking. These mindfulness methods will guide you and your team towards achieving this highly desirable, emotionally mature, and psychological approach.

You will know you have magnificently adopted Right-Minded attitudes and behaviors when the Right-Minded Teamwork motto of "**Do no harm** and **work as one**" comes easily to your team.

Along the way, you will most certainly create lasting trust, respect, and admiration among yourselves as well as between you and your team's customers.

This is the beauty of real-world team building. It unites teammates in achieving common goals.

Your team's act of uniting is your declaration of interdependence. It is your collective **moment of Reason** and your return to what we call the forgiving Unified Circle of Right-Minded Thinking.

When you join this Circle, you also join others who hold these mindful truths to be self-evident. Moreover, within this Circle, you know that all minds are created equal.

> *Whosoever believes in the oneness of equal minds will, undoubtedly, have everlasting freedom to always choose Right-Minded Teamwork.*

Most importantly, with Right-Minded Teamwork, you will actually resolve your team's problems and achieve customer satisfaction.

. . . . .

Welcome to Your New Role: RMT Leader & Facilitator

Now that you have a clearer sense of the journey we'll be taking together through these pages, I want to take a moment to congratulate you on your new role. Incorporating the 5 Elements into your team-building repertoire means **you are now a Right-Minded Teamwork Leader and Facilitator.**

As an RMT Leader and Facilitator, **your specialty is team transformations**.

Using RMT, you help to transform dysfunctional souls into healthy and functional teammates. You guide teammates to convert their mistakes into Right-Minded attitudes and behaviors. They express their deep and heartfelt gratitude for your facilitation efforts and results. Some even say you "saved them," continuing to seek your support for years to come.

Whether you're new to team leadership or team facilitation or not, add RMT to your team-building toolkit today. There's no reason not to: All parts of Right-Minded Teamwork, including the 5 Element Framework and Team Work Agreements, are available for your use. There are no licensing or certification requirements.

My only request is that you accept Reason's wisdom on this path. With Reason's guidance, you can easily apply these methods to help your client teams create and sustain Right-Minded Teamwork.

My Special Support Function

It took countless workshops, a 35-year career in active team-building facilitation, and the collective wisdom of so many teammates and team leaders to conceptualize and build Right-Minded Teamwork into the robust model it is today.

Though I no longer facilitate actively, choosing to pass that torch on to the next generation of leaders and facilitators, I will always continue to promote Right-Minded Teamwork.

The reason for my continued passion is quite simple. I know, beyond a shadow of a doubt, that RMT's 5 Elements and Team Work Agreements are right for every team, everywhere, forever. If you use them, they *will* help make your client team(s) and the world a better place.

To make that happen, though, **your clients need you to show them and their teams the Right-Minded Teamwork way.**

As you lead them down the RMT path, remember: I am here to support you. So, reach out to me. Ask me questions. Let me get to know you so I can refer you to clients looking for an RMT Leader or Facilitator.

Also remember that even though you will undoubtedly help your teams achieve an "early win," creating and sustaining Right-Minded Teamwork takes at least a year.

So, as you enter into the team-building process, stick with it for the long haul. Plan to stay with your team(s) for at least one to two years. Help them firmly establish RMT in their team. Give them the foundation they need to learn, grow, and succeed.

As you do, you will do your part to make the world a better place for everyone, everywhere, forever.

Let's get started now.

Dan Hogan

5 Elements of Right-Minded TEAMWORK

Right-Minded Teamwork's 5 Elements Framework: Overview

The Right-Minded Teamwork (RMT) model consists of five essential components or elements, incorporated into a core framework. Once you understand RMT's 5 Elements, it will be clear how applying RMT will help you overcome team obstacles to benefit your team and your team's customers.

The framework's 5 Elements include two goals and three methods:

1. Team **Business Goal**: Achieve 100% Customer Satisfaction

2. Team **Psychological Goal**: Commit to Right-Minded Thinking

3. Team **Work Agreements**: Create & Follow Commitments

4. **Team Operating System**: Make It Effective & Efficient

5. **Right-Minded Teammates**: Strengthen Individual Performance

Goal setting is the very first step of the Right-Minded Teamwork process. The first two elements provide goal-setting direction and a way to measure progress and success.

According to RMT, there are two types of goals every team should consider:

1. Business goals
2. Psychological goals

Without clear goals on both fronts, team members may falter, become distracted, or fail to fulfill their roles and responsibilities.

In addition to its two goal-setting elements, RMT also provides three specific team-building tools:

3. Work Agreements
4. Team Operating System
5. Right-Minded Teammate Development

Together, these tools create a strong, flexible, high-performing team ready to achieve ***your team goals***.

What Is "Right" in Right-Minded Teamwork?

RMT has nothing to do with right-brain thinking or right-wing viewpoints.

It has everything to do with what your team, together, decides is "right." Your team's choices, identified collectively, define your team's Right-Minded Teamwork.

The "right" way is the way you choose is right for your team.

So, how do you open up a team discussion about what is right or wrong for your team?

- ✓ You learn about Right-Minded Teamwork through this book, and you introduce it to your team.
- ✓ You apply some or all of the tools and exercises offered here.
- ✓ Then, you watch your team come together to work as one while doing no harm.

But for right now, all you need to do is continue reading.

How RMT's 5 Elements Work Together

Here's an overarching view of how RMT's 5 Elements work together.

For a team to succeed, each team member must first know, understand, and choose to align with the team's overarching performance goal (their business goal).

All team members must also remember, understand, and choose to align with the team's interpersonal, behavioral, and communication objectives (their psychological goals).

Recognizing each team member's value as part of the whole allows everyone to contribute fully and willingly, no matter their role. By clarifying and communicating both business and psychological goals, all team members are given a level playing field.

With clear goals in place, RMT's three tools can now be effectively applied to achieve those goals.

Firstly, Work Agreements, created collectively by all team members, ensure everyone operates under a single set of performance and behavioral expectations. Work Agreements are powerfully effective at resolving interpersonal issues and conflicts. To create your own team Work Agreements, consider using the Right-Minded Choice Model and its list of 30 Right-Minded Teamwork Attitudes & Behaviors, which will be introduced in Element #2.

Just as Work Agreements guide team behavior, the Team Operating System defines (or redefines) the team's structure. The Team Operating System includes roles, responsibilities, and team processes and procedures. You will learn more about this process in Element #4.

Lastly, Right-Minded Teammate Development offers teams a way forward by encouraging team members to focus on their individual and collective success. As you will learn in Element #5, Right-Minded Teammates support and encourage one another to reach new heights.

By applying the goals and tools of Right-Minded Teamwork's 5 Elements, you will set in place a continuous improvement loop with the power to revolutionize your team.

For a downloadable copy of RMT's 5 Element Model, go to RightMindedTeamwork.com, and search for this book's companion *Reusable Resources & Templates*.

RMT's 5 Elements & 12-Step Workshop Design Process

As a team leader, you have two options for applying RMT's 5 Elements within your team. You can facilitate the process yourself, or you can engage a team-building facilitator.

No matter which path you choose, you will increase the likelihood of a successful team-building event by using RMT's 12 Steps to Design a Right-Minded, Team-Building Workshop. If you choose to hire a facilitator, ask them to follow RMT's 12 Steps.

First, let's look at the standard Implementation Plan for RMT's 5 Elements. Then we'll take a closer look at the 12 Steps for creating effective team workshops.

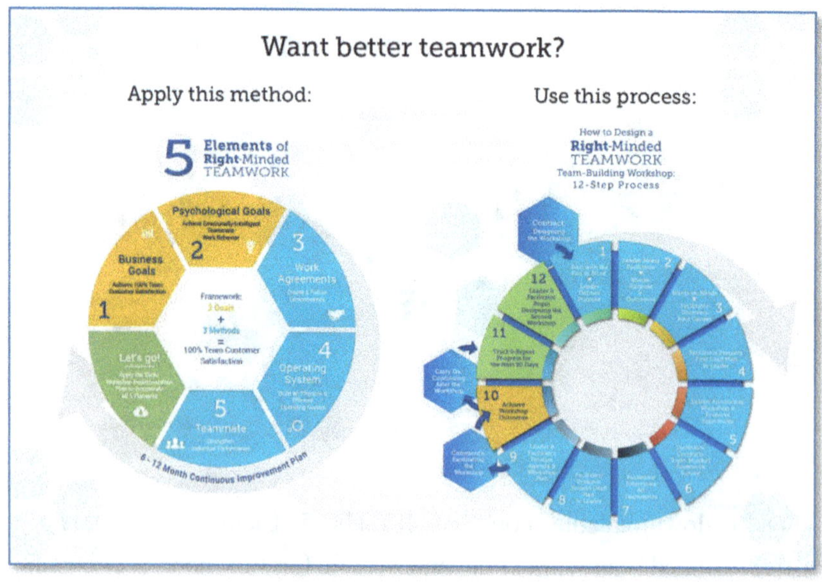

RMT's 5 Elements
Implementation Plan

Three Workshops + 90-Day Operating System

Overview

There is no one right way to implement RMT in your team; however, the three-workshop plan presented here has proven effective countless times.

These sequential actions will ensure you succeed in creating a *team that works together as one.*

Workshop Preparation & Team Orientation Meeting

- Team Leader & Facilitator prepare for team orientation
- Conduct a short Team Orientation meeting and assign teammate preparation tasks

First Workshop – Work Agreements

- Identify team psychological goals and values (Element #2)
- Create at least one team Work Agreement (Element #3)
- Identify 2 or 3 improvement projects for the next 90 days

Second Workshop – Operating System

- Reset and reaffirm business goals (Element #1) and agree on the Team Operating System (Element #4)

Third Workshop - Teammates

- Conduct a Right-Minded Teammate development workshop (Element #5).

90-Day Operating Plan - Ongoing

- Every 90 days, conduct another *Team Performance Factor Assessment,* and then the team meets to assess progress, identify opportunities, take action, and achieve new teamwork improvements.

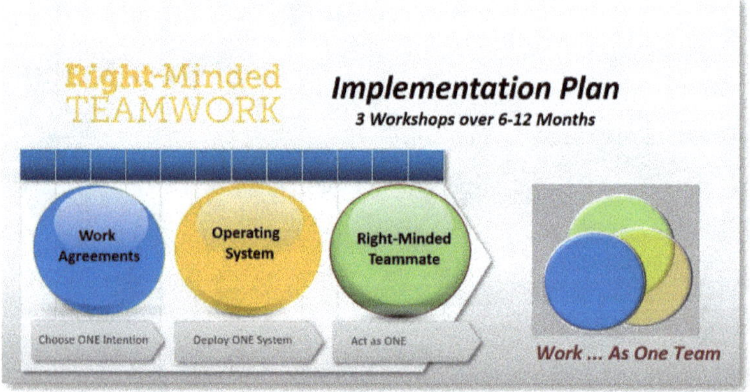

Workshop Preparation & Team Orientation Meeting

The team leader and the team-building facilitator will prepare for their team's RMT Team Orientation meeting and then conduct the meeting.

They will determine whether to conduct an in-person event or a virtual workshop. If they hold a virtual workshop, the same principles, concepts, and steps apply.

However, **an in-person workshop is highly recommended**. Being physically in the same room gives teammates a chance to see and feel other teammates' attitudes and behaviors.

If a virtual format is necessary, use a video software conferencing platform to ensure all participants can see each other and the virtual flip chart you will use to capture your team Work Agreements.

It's essential as one of your first steps to assess your team's current performance. This could be a subjective or an objective assessment. The facilitator will offer using the RMT *Team Performance Factor Assessment* that is discussed in Element #4 – Team Operating System.

In the orientation meeting, teammates will discuss and understand the RMT 5 Element process, the three-workshop implementation, the 90-day ongoing process, and the creation of team Work Agreements that will help them improve their teamwork.

Teammates learn the facilitator will guide the team in the first three workshops and co-facilitate their fourth. At that time, the facilitator will turn over the facilitation duties to the team going forward.

The leader and facilitator will facilitate a team discussion about choosing the teammate's two or three teamwork topics to address in their first workshop. Teammates learn the facilitator will interview them before the first workshop, and collectively, they will finalize the first topics to address. They also agree on the first workshop date.

Teammates are asked to read ***Right-Minded Teamwork**: 9 Right Choices for Building a Team That Works as One*. Doing so is optional, but this short and easy-to-read book will help foster an attitude of "Right-Mindedness" among all teammates.

Workshop 1 – Psychological Goals & Work Agreements

Under your leader or a facilitator's guidance, your team works together to clarify and agree on its psychological goals or team values and create one or more Work Agreements. Work Agreements, created collectively by and agreed upon by all team members, ensure everyone operates under a single set of performance and behavioral expectations. They are powerfully effective at resolving interpersonal issues and work process conflicts.

When your team creates and follows its first set of Agreements, it is an "early win" for the team because teammates resolve essential issues while also setting a positive, we-can-do-this tone for future successes.

Here's a real "early win" story. Look for **Example #3 – International Project Team**, in the RMT Implementation Plan – 4 Actual Examples section at the end of this book. This major capital project team immediately saved $10,000 a week in labor costs when they successfully used RMT's **process Work Agreement** to streamline their meetings. Furthermore, all four examples will show you clear evidence that Work Agreements work.

But to help you on your way to achieving an “early win,” you can **use the list of 30 Right-Minded attitudes**, discussed in this book in Element #2 – Psychological Goal, to help you choose your team's goals and desired work behaviors.

The first workshop typically focuses on team cohesion and unity. Often a lack of cohesion or unity is the underlying cause of poor performance that created your team's improvement opportunities.

If your team is currently struggling with strained relationships or poor work processes, it may be best to obtain an external team-building facilitator. Ask them to apply RMT’s ***Design a Right-Minded, Team-Building Workshop*** process to create the agenda and facilitate Work Agreements in your first workshop.

Whether you retain an outside facilitator or choose to lead your own team-building workshop, teams often experience a boost in productivity and motivation from the first workshop alone because they immediately see the positive benefits of the Right-Minded Teamwork model.

Workshop 2 – Business Goals & Operating System

Once psychological goals and initial Work Agreements are in place, you are ready for the second workshop. This event revolves around clarifying your business goal and establishing an effective Team Operating System.

Often, the business goal is to achieve 100% customer satisfaction. If so, your team must agree on what this kind of success looks like for your clients. Additionally, it is crucial that you validate your conclusions with your team's customers.

Validating your assumptions means ensuring all teammates know and understand not only the expectations of your team's direct customers but also the expectations of *their customers*.

> *When your team helps your customers achieve 100% satisfaction with* ***their customers****, you will most certainly have achieved a prosperous and successful working relationship.*

Note: in Element #1, you will find instructions in this section: **Steps for Creating a Customer Satisfaction Plan.**

With a clear business goal and united focus, you are ready to discuss and create an actionable plan to strengthen work performance and eliminate wasted time and effort.

In this second team-building workshop, you will identify one to three opportunities to improve your **Team Operating System** over the next 90 days.

Just as Work Agreements guide team behavior, the Team Operating System defines (or redefines) your team's structure. The system includes a *Team Performance Factor Assessment* that helps your team identify improvement opportunities such as roles, responsibilities, and team processes and procedures. In Element #4, you will learn more about RMT's 90-Day Team Operating System and how to use it.

This second workshop continues to build momentum by delivering more evidence that the RMT model is working.

For a downloadable copy of the Team Operating Model, go to RightMindedTeamwork.com, and search for *Reusable Resources & Templates* for **Right-Minded Teamwork in Any Team**.

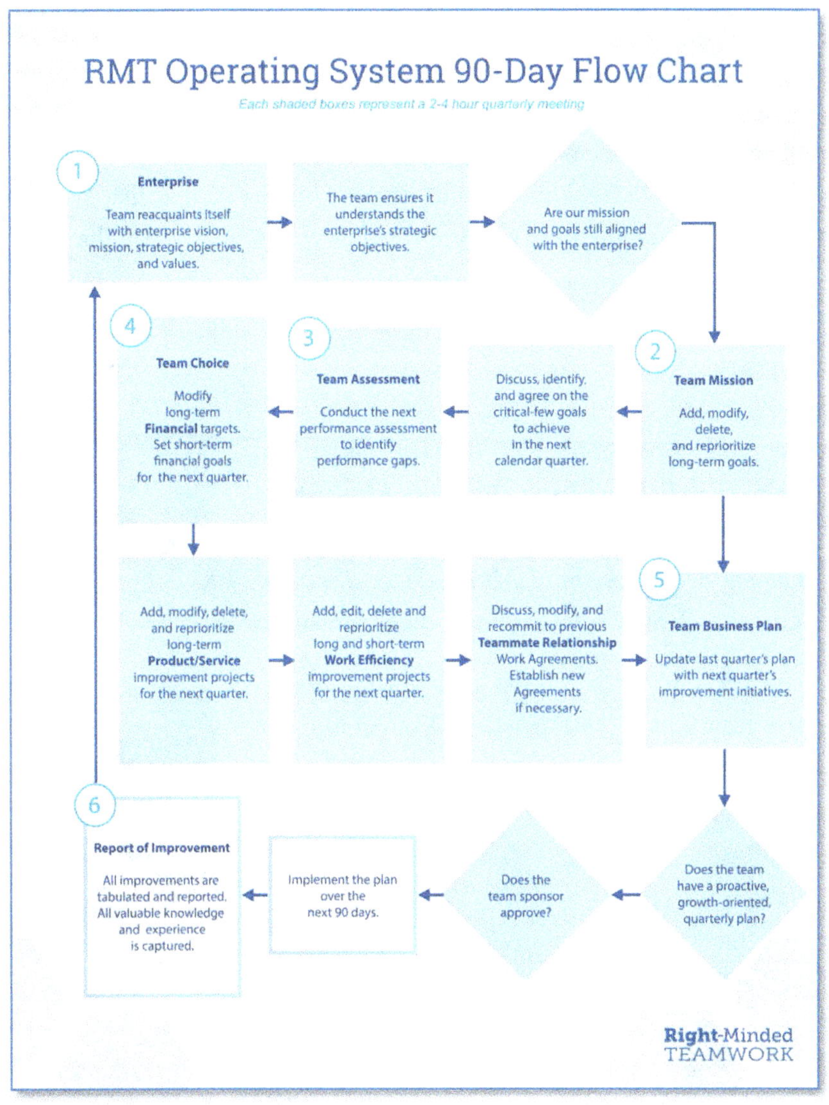

Workshop 3 – Teammate Growth & Development

Now that teammates have experienced more productive teamwork from the first two workshops, you are ready to conduct the third workshop focused on individual growth and development.

In this workshop, teammates are encouraged to take an honest look at their attitudes, behaviors, and work performance. They are asked to identify simple, legitimate, and actional improvements that will not only improve individual performance but will help improve the team's collective performance. Improvement goals are then shared with teammates to not only validate them but to encourage wholehearted support.

For this workshop, you have a variety of training options. You might choose to instruct teammates more thoroughly in RMT's ***Right Choice Model*** or the ***7 Mindfulness Training Lessons***. You could invite a professional to teach a new work process that would enhance the team's work efficiencies. You could also request a behavioral training specialist to teach such things as how to communicate during conflicts.

The outcome of this workshop is to identify actionable improvements for each person.

After you complete your third RMT workshop, you and your teammates will be totally convinced that your Team Operating System, Work Agreements, and customer satisfaction mission will ensure you create and sustain Right-Minded Teamwork.

Approximately 90 days after your third workshop (and every 90 days after that), your team will follow your Team Operating Plan (created in the second workshop) to assess team progress, identify new improvement opportunities, take action, and achieve greater team success.

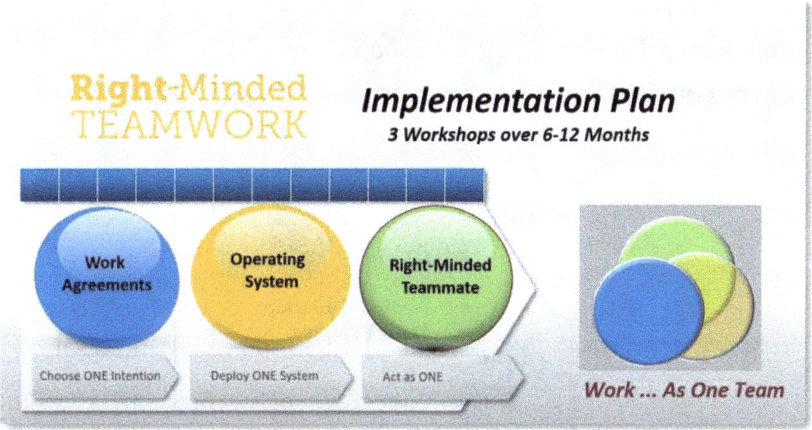

90-Day Operating Plan - Ongoing

- Every 90 days, conduct another *Team Performance Factor Assessment,* and then the team meets to assess progress, identify opportunities, take action, and achieve new teamwork improvements.

To Learn More...

For four real-world success stories illustrating this multi-workshop plan, go to the Resources section at the end of this book and find ***RMT Implementation Plan – 4 Actual Examples****.*

How to Design a Right-Minded, Team-Building Workshop

Ready to design your own transformational real-world team-building workshop? RMT's proven, repeatable process involves three phases or segments:

Contract: Designing the workshop - Steps 1-9
Commence: Facilitating the workshop - Step 10
Carry On: Continuing after the workshop - Steps 11-12

The 12 Steps are as follows:

Step 1 – Start with the end in mind: the leader's purpose

Step 2 – Leader shares the purpose and outcomes with the facilitator

Step 3 – The leader's wants and the team's needs might be different

Step 4 – Facilitator presents leader with 1st draft team-building plan

Step 5 – Leader announces workshop and prepares teammates

Step 6 – Facilitator conducts Right-Minded Teammate Survey

Step 7 – The facilitator interviews all teammates

Step 8 – Facilitator presents leader with 2nd draft team-building plan

Step 9 – Leader & facilitator finalize and distribute workshop agenda

Step 10 – Facilitator and leader conduct the team-building workshop

Step 11 – Team implements Improvement Plan and tracks the results

Step 12 – Leader and facilitator begin designing next team workshop

5 Elements of Right-Minded TEAMWORK
1
Business Goals
Achieve 100% Team Customer Satisfaction
2
Psychological Goals
Achieve Emotionally-Intelligent Teammate Work Behavior
3
Work Agreements
Create and Follow Commitments
4
Operating System
Build an Effective & Efficient Operating System
5
Teammate
Strengthen Individual Performance
Let's go!
Apply the Three Workshop Implementation Plan to incorporate all 5 Elements
Framework:
2 Goals
+
3 Methods
=
100% Team Customer Satisfaction
6 - 12 Month Continuous Improvement Plan

RMT's 5 Elements: A Detailed Description

Now that we've shared an overview of the 5 Elements and how they can be applied in a series of three consecutive workshops, conducted over the course of six to 12 months and designed using RMT's 12 Steps workshop approach, let's take a more detailed look at each of RMT's 5 Elements and how they integrate to help you level up your team.

Element #1
Business Goal: 100% Customer Satisfaction

Clear goals focus your team.

For your team to succeed, each team member must first know, understand, and choose to align with the team's overarching performance goals, including its vision, mission, and charter.

Said another way, your team is responsible for providing products or services to customers. For the team and the enterprise to succeed, those customers must be satisfied, ideally 100% of the time. It is up to you and your team to identify the processes and behaviors that will get you there - the "right" way for your team. Additionally, teammates must see how their efforts contribute to the team's goals in order to be motivated to help achieve them.

Since 100% customer satisfaction is a universal goal for teams, RMT focuses on guiding teams to achieve this business goal.

Within the 5 Elements framework that forms Right-Minded Teamwork, the team business goal is the first Element. This segment of RMT advocates two tasks:

1. Ask your customers what 100% satisfaction means to them and create a plan to achieve it.
2. Make sure all team business goals align with your organization's strategic plan.

Without clear, aligned goals, team members may falter, become distracted, or fail to fulfill their roles on the team. Identifying your team's business goal gets your team on the same page.

Create & Implement a Team Customer Satisfaction Plan

The primary reason for your team's existence is to meet or exceed your team's customers' expectations. Creating a high-performing team that does this is also undoubtedly essential, but it is secondary.

Therefore, your team's first business goal is to create a plan for how teammates will deliver what your customers expect.

When your teammates clearly understand what will satisfy your customers and how they help make that happen, they can make the conscious choice to follow your team-building practices and chosen work behaviors.

Steps for Creating a Customer Satisfaction Plan

These simple, practical steps will help you create a strong customer satisfaction plan.

1. As an entire team, discuss and agree on a set of specific questions to ask your customers. Here are five excellent suggestions.

    a. What are the essential products or services you need from us?
    b. What are *your customer's expectations of your team*, and how does our team help you achieve those expectations?
    c. Where are we meeting or exceeding your expectations?
    d. Where are we NOT meeting your expectations?
    e. Is there anything we are giving you now that you do not need?

2. Choose two teammates who will conduct customer interviews.

3. Ask permission to interview your customers. Give them the questions before the interview so they can prepare.

4. Conduct the interviews.
    a. Take notes. At the end of the interview, reflect back to them what you heard them say. This "reflection" or paraphrasing ensures alignment. This is how you validate your Customer Satisfaction Plan.
    b. Ask, "If we consistently delivered those products or services, would you be 100% satisfied?"
    c. Also, ask, "May we come back in 90 days for another customer satisfaction performance review?"

5. As a whole team, discuss the results of the customer interviews.
   a. Teammates need to ask clarifying questions to understand what they must start, stop, or continue doing.

6. Based on this information, teammates discuss and agree on a Customer Satisfaction Plan, which may include modifying individual teammate roles and responsibilities to better align with customer satisfaction.

7. All teammates agree and commit to doing their part to achieve 100% customer satisfaction.

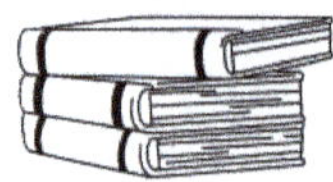

To Learn More…

Your Team Has a Dissatisfied Customer

In the RMT book, ***How To Apply the Right Choice Model**: Create a Right-Minded Team That Works as One*, you will find an excellent example of how an Accounts Payable Department learned about and then successfully addressed a dissatisfied customer.

The story is in this section: *How to Present & Apply the Right Choice Model in Your Team.*

Align Team Business Goals with the Organization's Strategic Plan

Once a Customer Satisfaction Plan is in place, this strategy should be added to the team's current set of business goals.

The team leader will then schedule a goal alignment meeting with their supervisor. In that meeting, the team leader will:

- present all the team's business goals
- discuss and adjust any misaligned goals
- commit to making demonstrable progress toward achieving those goals.

With team business goals clarified and aligned with the organization's vision and strategic plan, it's now time to ensure that team member behaviors and interactions – RMT's Element #2 – are also aligned.

5 Elements of Right-Minded TEAMWORK

Element #2
Psychological Goal: Right-Minded Thinking

Right-Minded Teamwork advocates a psychological approach to team building. Here's why:

> *Your thoughts precede and cause your work behavior.*
>
> *Therefore, when you consistently choose Right-Minded thoughts and attitudes, your work behavior will also shift, which naturally improves teamwork.*

Commit to Your Team's Version of Right-Minded Thinking

Psychological goals illustrate how your team's behavior and Work Agreements align with your organization's stated values.

To achieve Right-Minded Teamwork, your team must first identify the "right" attitudes for the team. These chosen attitudes form your team's collective, consciously chosen thought system. They describe how you will **Do No Harm** as you **Work as One**.

Your team's initial set of Right-Minded Teamwork attitudes is created and agreed upon during the first RMT team-building workshop. After that, they may be adjusted and updated on an as-needed basis.

How to Choose Right-Minded Attitudes for Your Team

Your list of "right" attitudes can be short. Here is an example.

We choose these Right-Minded attitudes as our psychological goals:

- *We accept 100% accountability and responsibility for our thoughts and behaviors.*
- *When we make mistakes, we never punish. We learn. We recover. We do no harm. We work as one.*
- *We positively acknowledge and reward each other.*
- *We are we-centered, never self-centered.*
- *When difficult team situations happen, we accept, forgive, and adjust our attitudes and behavior. We always find solutions because we believe that none of us is as smart as all of us.*
- *When new teammates join our team, we will share these goals and ask them to choose them too.*

After you create these values and norms for your team, you must commit to living them. Both the attitudes and the team's commitment to living them are captured in your team's Work Agreements.

Two Options for Choosing Attitudes & Behaviors

To identify the "right" attitudes and psychological goals for your team, you have two options:

1. Share the **Right-Minded Teammate Attitudes & Behaviors** list with the team; see below and allow teammates to choose a few from that list. Or use those ideas to create goals that fit your team better.

2. Share the **Right Choice Model** (as described in the book ***How to Apply the Right Choice Model:*** *Create a Right-Minded Team That Works as One.* In a team event, agree on a list of accountable attitudes and work behaviors your team believes are needed to address your teamwork issues and sustain RMT successfully.

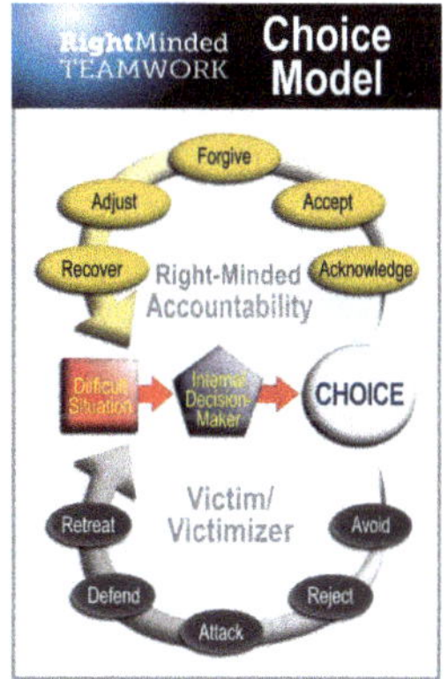

To Learn More…

To learn more about presenting and teaching the Right Choice Model, go to RightMindedTeamwork.com or your favorite book retailer and pick up your copy of ***How to Apply the Right Choice Model****: Create a Right-Minded Team That Works as One*. Search for the section, "*How to Present & Apply the Right Choice Model in Your Team.*"

You Have Only Two Response Choices

The Right-Minded Teamwork Choice Model teaches that you are the Decision-Maker, and you only have two choices regarding how you respond to every difficult situation.

When a challenging situation happens, you either:

1. accept Ego's guidance and act like a victim or victimizer, or
2. embrace Reason and act in an accountable, Right-Minded way.

Though there are many variations of those two choices, there are still just two.

At all times, you are mindful, or you are mindless. You are either following your Right Mind, Reason, or your wrong mind, Ego.

For the background story behind the RMT Choice Model, read RMT's ***Reason, Ego, and the Right-Minded Teamwork Myth***. This story introduces the three characters who live in every teammate's life: Reason, Ego, and the Decision-Maker.

You Are the Decision-Maker

The Right-Minded Choice Model says "you" are your own internal Decision-Maker.

This "you" is your observer, interpreter, and decider. It is the part of you that sees all your experiences and determines how you will respond to those situations.

Look closely at the Right Choice Model now.

Do you see yourself, the Decision-Maker, sitting right in the middle between your difficult situation and the choice you must make?

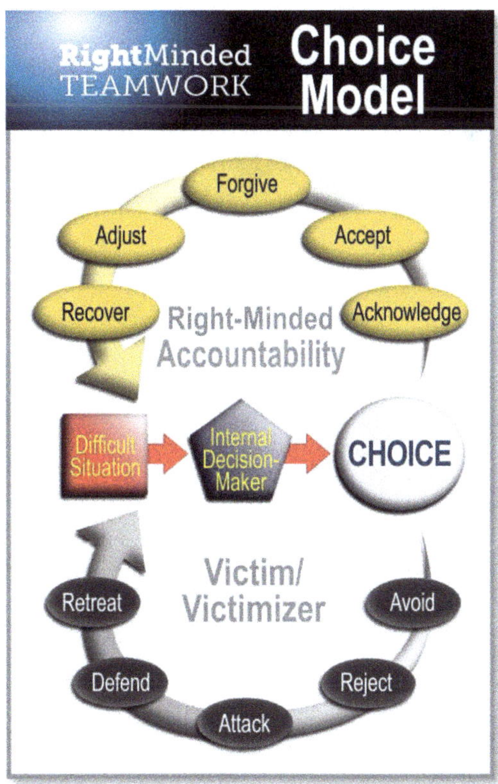

In this position, between the difficult situation you are facing and the choice you must make, you are faced with two choices. You either choose the right direction, as described in your Work Agreements, or the wrong direction.

As the Decision-Maker, you are never alone during these moments of choice.

Reason and Ego are always there in your mind, every time you make choices, whether you are conscious of them or not. Each time you make a decision, you either mindfully and consciously choose to follow Reason's Right-Minded attitudes, or you mindlessly and unconsciously decide to follow Ego's lessons and wrong-minded thinking.

Choosing the upper loop means **accepting**, **forgiving**, and **adjusting**, which is your mindful move into the Unified Circle of Right-Minded Thinking. In contrast, the lower loop of rejection, Ego attack, and defensiveness describes the divided circle of wrong-minded thinking.

Right-Minded Teamwork upholds the upper circle.

For more about Right-Minded attitudes, see the Right-Minded Teamwork Attitudes & Behaviors list below.

Trust Your Intuition as the Decision-Maker

If thinking about Reason and Ego is new to you, it can be helpful to think of Reason as your positive intuition and Ego as your negative, arrogant, and sometimes vindictive intuition.

At different times throughout our lives, we all listen to and follow each of these teachers.

Stop and remember when you had a hunch or a feeling as to what you should do or say in a particular situation. Did you ignore your intuition? Let's say you did not follow your instinct, and it turned out to be a mistake. What did you say to yourself and others?

I wish I had trusted my intuition!

As this memory illustrates, **you already know how to listen and be mindful** of your intuition. It is your natural pre-separation state of mind. You just need to do it regularly.

If not…

Remember a time when you became angry, agitated, or annoyed with a teammate. Without thinking, you said mean-spirited things. You, too, were saying to yourself, *"My life can't get better until you change."* Accept it. Your negative behavior happened because you did not stop for a **moment of Reason.**

You were literally **out of your Right Mind** as you unconsciously turned towards Ego for guidance.

During your reaction, you were mindless as you followed **Ego's advice**. Then, after a while, once you stepped back and calmed down, you could see your behavior was a mistake - only a mistake, to be corrected, not punished. At this moment, you shifted your perspective. You forgave yourself, and you adjusted by apologizing and promising not to behave that way again. You returned to your Right Mind.

If you are not accustomed to trusting your intuition but would like to do so more, you will need to practice.

> *The key is to **pause**, be **still**, and intentionally **listen** for your positive intuition - that **moment of Reason** - before you react to a situation or event.*

It is that simple. But that does not make it easy, especially at first. It takes mindful practice to *train your mind* to listen for this joyous, intuitive moment. It takes an unwavering commitment to stop yourself continually, gently, and compassionately when you become angry, fearful, agitated, or anxious.

It is not always easy, but it can be done. Many have learned this skill. You can, too. As the Decision-Maker, you always have free will regarding whether you choose to follow Ego or Reason. Even if you've tried before and failed, you can start again today.

Remember that even with steadfast commitment, it will take practice to excel. You will make mistakes. That's okay. Choose Reason again. Choose to follow your Work Agreements again. And again. When you realize you've chosen Ego, apologize, forgive, correct, forget the mistake and move on. The more you practice, the easier it will get.

You will soon find that as you change your mind, you automatically change your behavior. And when you change your behavior, you transform your team into a lovely learning classroom. The more you make an effort to ***be in your Right Mind***, the easier it will become to ***stay in your Right Mind***.

Now, instead of saying, *"I wish I had listened to my intuition,"* you will say,

I'm so glad I turned ***towards*** *Reason and followed my intuition!*

Mindfulness Is Choice in Action

When you are mindless, you don't think or reflect. Instead of *consciously* choosing how to respond, you react *unconsciously* in an emotionally immature way, blaming others or avoiding the situation altogether.

When you're mindful, you reflect and carefully choose how you respond to everything that happens to you and around you. When a problematic situation happens, being mindful means asking yourself this question that is in the model:

What did I do or say to ***create, promote****, or* ***allow*** *this to happen?*

Your answers to this question help you and your team experience a **moment of Reason**, which paves the way for you to create real solutions.

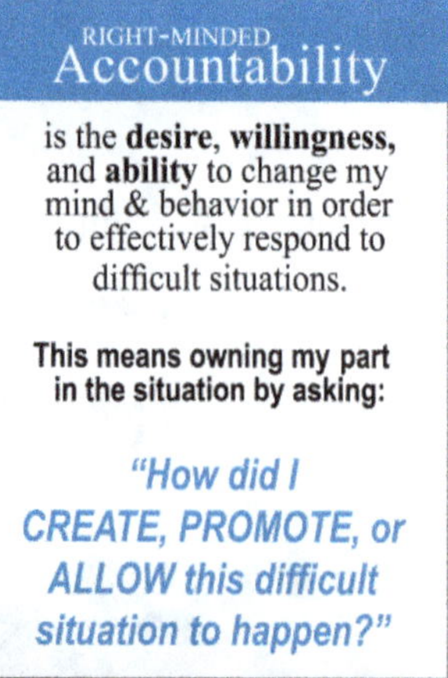

As an example, let's assume a significant mistake has happened in your team.

Half the team is aggressively blaming the other half for the mistake in what is often called an **"Ego attack."** Teammates are making toxic and hurtful statements, directly and indirectly, about each other. The team is stuck in a battleground of "attack and defend." No one is working to resolve the mistake.

Seeking a **moment of Reason**, you ask yourself,

> *What am I doing to create, promote, or allow this blaming conversation to continue?*

You realize you've been standing by and saying nothing. **You were avoiding**, which is the **first step in the lower loop** of the Right Choice Model.

Now that you are aware of your attitude and behavior, you change your mind. You choose to follow Reason and act in a Right-Minded, accountable way, just as your Work Agreement states.

Reason is that part of your mind that always speaks for the Right Choice Attitudes & Behaviors. When you need a **moment of Reason**, to find the best way to respond to a difficult team situation, say to yourself:

> *I am here to be truly helpful.*
>
> *I am here to represent Reason who sent me.*
>
> *I do not have to worry about what to say or what to do because Reason who sent me will direct me.*

You remember these two Right-Minded options:

1. Engage in helpful problem-solving communication.
2. Advocate that teammates correct mistakes rather than punish and blame.

As you reflect while holding these two choices in your mind and heart, ***intuitive*** answers come to your *"right"* mind. Now that you have received Reason's advice, in a calm, "do-no-harm-work-as-one" voice, you say,

> *Here's a suggestion. Let's discuss what we know, the facts, about what happened. Then let's find an immediate solution.*
>
> *After we resolve the mistake, let's have a second team discussion, not to blame, but to create a Work Agreement so that this mistake doesn't happen again. How does that sound?*

If you had followed Ego's advice and continued your **avoidance behavior**, the conflict would have continued. Since you chose to look towards Reason, you created an environment where you and your teammates **recovered** from the mistake, the **final step in the upper loop** of the model.

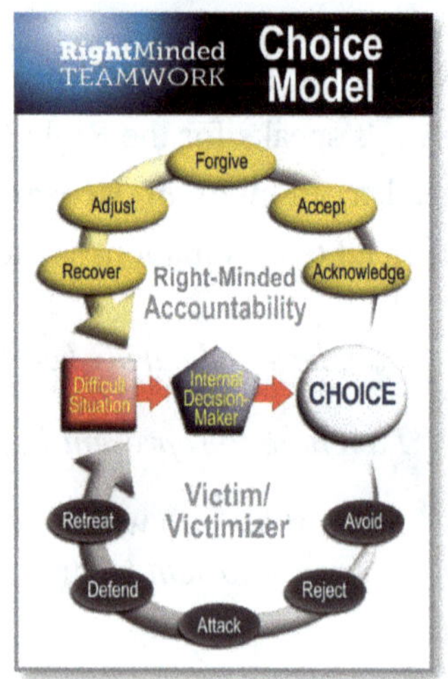

Reason, as always, has brought you - and hopefully everyone else, too - ***back into your Right Mind***.

By listening to Reason, trusting your intuition, and following your Work Agreements, you train your mind to consistently return to the Unified Circle of Right-Minded Thinking.

What Does It Mean to "Train Your Mind?"

When your mind is well-trained, and a difficult team situation happens, you immediately **stop for a moment of Reason.** You remember that you want to **live your Work Agreements**.

Training your mind simply means practicing your team's Work Agreements, which represent your psychological goals, as often as possible, especially during difficult team situations.

By actively asking the question "How did I **create**, **promote**, or **allow** this difficult situation to happen?" and then **stepping back in your mind** to listen for the answers, you will learn to hear and implicitly trust Reason's voice. The Right-Minded Teamwork tools and methods become catalysts that carry you deeper into your Right Mind, where you hear the best answers to the questions you ask.

Once you have those answers, you will always know how to behave and respond.

So, **how do you know** you are listening to the voice of Reason?

The **first** indication is a feeling of *inner peace*. **Secondly**, you will know you've heard Reason when *the answer you have received heals and resolves the difficulty* you face while doing no harm to anyone.

If your solution meets both of these criteria, rest assured you are listening to Reason and working as one.

Over time, as you train your mind, you forgive the errors and mistakes of yourself and your teammates by recognizing them, accepting them, and immediately moving toward finding solutions.

The Constantly Complaining Teammate (CCT)

Here's an example of how to **successfully train your mind**.

Think about a team experience where you've had to deal with a "CCT" - a Constantly Complaining Teammate.

In your mind, what do you picture when you see and interact with this person?

If what you see in your mind's eye is a big angry dog, ready to attack you and others, you are seeing the CCT through your Ego's eyes. You believe they are to be feared and avoided.

It is the perspective of an untrained and unforgiving mind. But it doesn't have to stay that way.

Alternatively, you can choose to follow Reason. When you genuinely desire to follow Reason's guidance, and you practice being mindful of your thoughts and choices, your perspective changes.

With Reason's help, instead of seeing your CCT as a vicious dog ready to attack, your new perception now shows you a cute-though-angry puppy. It is now *impossible* to fear them, and there is certainly no valid reason to avoid them.

With your new and healed perspective, you reinterpret the CCT's complaints as mistakes that need correction, not punishment. You accept their complaints as *their call for help,* not an attack.

Instead of reacting negatively, you say to yourself:

I will do my best to forgive this person for their constantly complaining behavior because I honestly think they care about doing a good job, even if they communicate poorly.

I will listen to their complaints. I'll ask clarifying questions to be sure I fully understand.

I will be kind, compassionate, non-judgmental, and civil in the way I respond. I will not get defensive. I will do no harm. I'll ask how we should resolve the situation.

When this Right-Minded perception shift happens, you will finally see your CCT for who they really are.

> *Rather than a person to be feared, avoided, harmed, or dismissed, your teammate is now a worthy sister or brother who wants to be heard, included, and helped – by YOU.*

They truly deserve no less than your Right-Minded, caring, and loving response.

Return to the Unified Circle of Right-Minded Thinking

When your team discusses and agrees on your psychological goals – your consciously chosen set of attitudes and behaviors as described in your Work Agreements – you have created your team's collective thought system.

By uniting with each other in this way and openly committing to one another through your Work Agreements, you are renouncing Ego in yourself and your teammates and collectively committing to train your minds to follow Reason.

This process of creating team Work Agreements is your undivided declaration of interdependence. Your assertion is saying,

> *We hold these mindful truths to be self-evident that all minds are created equal, and whosoever believes that will have everlasting freedom to choose Right-Minded teamwork.*

Your declaration plus your daily acts of living your team Work Agreements ***is your return*** to the forgiving Unified Circle of Right-Minded Thinking.

The one fundamental freedom that no one can take away from you is **your freedom to choose** how to respond to life's challenges.

At every moment, your Decision-Maker is making that choice in one of two ways: Either your Decision-Maker is choosing based on Reason's Right-Minded principles or Ego's wrong-minded dictates.

> *Follow Reason, and you declare your freedom from Ego's battlefields.*
>
> *Follow Reason, and you have joined others who hold these Right-Minded thoughts to be self-evident and true.*
>
> *Follow Reason, and you transform your fixed perspectives by reinterpreting attack behaviors as a call for help – your help.*
>
> *Follow Reason, and your team will agree on a Right-Minded set of attitudes and behaviors as described in your **Work Agreements.***
>
> *By following **Reason** and your **Work Agreements**, you will renounce Ego while uniting with your fellow teammates.*
>
> *When you do these, you will return to your ultimate goal, the forgiving Unified Circle of Right-Minded Thinking.*

Right-Minded Teamwork Attitudes & Behaviors

Over decades of team-building work, I worked with hundreds of teams. Along the way, I collected their Right-Minded attitudes and behaviors into a list of choices that I grouped into **work behaviors** and **work processes**. Use this list to either adopt or adapt your team's Psychological Goals and Work Agreements.

Was I Born With These Thoughts & Attitudes?

Thoughts and attitudes always precede teamwork behavior.

Right-Minded attitudes come from Reason. Wrong-minded attitudes come from Ego.

The good news is that Right-Minded attitudes are natural. They are already inside you and your teammates.

When you think about any of the wrong-minded Ego attitudes listed below, ask yourself,

> *Was I born with these depressing, debilitating, and awful attitudes?*

Your answer will always be "**no!**" You learned those wrong-minded attitudes from Ego. That means ***you can unlearn them, too.***

You *Can* Change Your Mind

In 35 years of team-building facilitation, I heard too many well-intentioned albeit wrong-minded teammates say,

> *That's just the way I am. I can't change.*

That is ***simply not true***.

What is true is that they refused to change their minds.

> *When someone says they cannot change, what they are really saying is their behavior is more powerful than their mind.*

When they realize and joyfully accept that ***their mind is in charge***, they have opened the way for happiness, inner peace, and Right-Minded Teamwork.

Why You Want to Change Your Perspective

Fixed perspectives prevent you from achieving Right-Minded Teamwork. Your limiting beliefs, interpretations, and lessons from Ego are blocks to Right-Minded Thinking.

To remove those blocks, you must transform your self-limiting thoughts. The first of RMT's 7 Mindfulness Training Lessons will help you do that.

Lesson one of the 7 Mindfulness Training Lessons states, *"I am never upset for the reason I think."*

Reminding yourself of this truth when you or your teammates are out of your Right Minds will help you experience a **moment of Reason**. Instead of seeing your teammate's behavior as a negative Ego attack, you are able to reinterpret their behavior as a desperate **call for help** from you and your teammates.

With this new insight, you are able to respond to your teammate with Reason's wise guidance. With Reason's help, you have effectively changed your perspective.

. . . . .

The 30 Right-Minded Teamwork Attitudes & Behaviors starting on the next page will help you change your perspective and achieve Right-Minded Thinking.

Work Behavior Attitudes

As the Decision-Maker, You Behave One Way or the Other!

Demonstrate adversarial competition and power struggles	Demonstrate collaborative competition and synergy
Demonstrate victim or victimizer attitudes & behaviors	Exhibit accountable and responsible attitudes & behavior
Worry that "I am my mistakes;" continue to obsess over mistakes	Embrace that "I am not my mistakes;" mistakes are opportunities for me to learn
Noticeable lack of emotional maturity and empathy	Desire to be emotionally mature and compassionate
Exhibit self-centered attitudes	Exhibit we-centered attitudes
Hold & project grievances; Never forget or forgive	Embrace & extend forgiveness; Let go of issues from the past
After mistakes, helplessness occurs, and I choose to give up or not try as hard	After mistakes, forgiveness occurs, and I choose to try again and again

Work Behavior Attitudes (Continued)

There's a mindset of scarcity, a belief that to give is to lose	There's an attitude of abundance, a belief that to give is to receive
There is suspicion, closed-mindedness, and resistance to change	There is readiness and open-mindedness for positive change
Too often, people restate their position, believing they are right, and others are wrong	We always seek mutual understanding: believing together, we are right
I believe I'm the smartest, and I can prove it	We believe none of us is as smart as all of us
I demonstrate a conscious or unconscious attitude of confusion, chaos, complexity, and drama	We continually demonstrate a conscious attitude of clarity, order, simplicity, and calmness
There's a widespread belief that difficult team situations and changes determine how we feel	We know for sure that our minds determine how we feel about difficult situations or changes
We believe it is best to keep quiet when correction is needed	We have a team culture of appropriately speaking up when a correction is needed
We believe in these attitudes: vulnerability, unkindness, hate, attack, blame	We embrace these attitudes: invulnerability, love, kindness, do no harm, work as one

Work Behavior Attitudes (Continued)

We believe in power over others	We believe in power with others
Growth is painful; remember, if there is no pain, there is no gain	Growth doesn't have to be painful; learning is joyously attained and gladly remembered
It is best to do unto others (reject, attack, defend) before they do unto you	We do unto others (accept, forgive, adjust) as we would have them do unto us
There is a feeling of avoidance and criticism among teammates	There is a spirit of acknowledgment and reward among teammates
There is a love and a need for power, fame, money, and pleasure	We strive for non-attachment to power, fame, money, and pleasure
Our team is a battleground where conflict is prolonged as we act like victims or victimizers	Our team is our learning classroom where conflict is resolved as we act like Right-Minded Teammates
There is mistrust, fear, and lack of safety among teammates	There is trust, peace, and safety among teammates
Defensiveness is prevalent in our team	Defenselessness is widespread in our team

Process Behavior Attitudes

Your Team Can Operate One Way or the Other!

The team's purpose, vision, and mission are unclear and not supported	Our team continuously clarifies our purpose, vision, and mission and actively support them
There is no discernable team operating system	There is an efficient, continuous improvement team operating system in place
There is a predominant attitude of avoidance and complaining	We have an attitude and a system for acknowledgment and reward
Disagreements and a lack of clear roles and responsibilities exist	We periodically clarify teammate roles and responsibilities
We are unclear who makes decisions and how	Our team has a clear and effective decision-making Work Agreement
We spend too much time and energy applying inefficient work processes	Our work processes and procedures are clear, understood, accepted, and efficient
Too often, people are punished for making mistakes	We always embrace an attitude of converting mistakes into learning opportunities

Actionable Attitudes = Better Behaviors

These Right-Minded attitudes are practical. However, these noble thoughts and attitudes will do no good unless you discuss them and define what they mean for your team.

Once you have identified and defined the behaviors associated with your chosen attitudes, captured in your team Work Agreements, you must also make the conscious choice to live them going forward.

Don't let your team's insignificant, Ego-driven squabbles pull you down.

Be vigilant and demonstrate by your actions and behaviors that you have risen above your old, petty, teamwork battleground issues.

No team situation can pull you into Ego's realm of conflict when you believe it is far better to collaborate and win than argue and lose.

Remember, it is from your collective Right Mind that you create your Work Agreements. And when you make and follow your promises, you are uniting with each other without the Ego. When you do that, you have returned to the United Circle of Right-Minded Thinking. From that unified circle, it will be much easier to recover from any difficult team situation because you have, at that moment, restored your team's collective Right Mind to Reason.

7 Mindfulness Training Lessons

In addition to using the **Right Choice Model** and the **RMT Attitudes & Behaviors** list to strengthen your team's Right-Minded Thinking, you can also read and apply RMT's ***7 Mindfulness Training Lessons***.

Right-Minded Teammates use these lessons to consistently choose a Right-Minded way of thinking and behaving.

The seven lessons from this book can be summed up in just one sentence, with emphasis on three specific words:

Right-Minded Teammates **accept**, **forgive**, and **adjust** their thinking and work behavior.

To start applying these lessons in your life and team, go to RightMindedTeamwork.com or your favorite book retailer, and pick up your copy of ***7 Mindfulness Training Lessons****: Improve Teammates' Ability to Work as One with Right-Minded Thinking.*

The 10 Characteristics of Right-Minded Teammates

And yet one more resource is the Ten Characteristics of Right-Minded Teammates for strengthening Right-Minded Thinking.

1. Trust	2. Honesty	3. Tolerance
4. Gentleness	5. Joy	6. Defenselessness
7. Generosity	8. Patience	9. Open-Mindedness
	10. Faithfulness	

You can find the **full explanation** of these in **Element #5 below**.

Align Team Psychological Goals with the Organization's Values

Just as the team leader presents the team's business goal of 100% customer satisfaction to their supervisor, the team leader should also review the team's new psychological goals (the team's Work Agreements) and plan for achieving them with the team leader's supervisor.

If timed right, a review of both business and psychological goals can coincide.

In that goal alignment meeting, the team leader will:

- present the team's business and psychological goals
- discuss and adjust any misaligned goals
- commit to making demonstrable progress toward achieving those goals.

With clear, unified business and psychological goals, the team has completed the first two Elements of RMT's 5 Elements framework. The team is now ready to apply the final three team-building tools: **Work Agreements**, the **Team Operating System**, and **Right-Minded Teammate Development.**

These methods will ensure your team achieves its business and psychological goals.

Now let's move on to Element #3: Work Agreements.

5 Elements of Right-Minded TEAMWORK

Element #3
Work Agreements: Create & Follow Commitments

In this book's preface, I shared the following RMT definition:

> *Right-Minded Teamwork is a business-oriented, psychological approach to team building where **acceptance**, **forgiveness**, and **adjustment** are teammate characteristics, and 100% customer satisfaction is the team's result.*

When you apply RMT, you create Work Agreements that describe your team's behavioral characteristics of ***acceptance***, ***forgiveness***, and ***adjustment***.

Your Work Agreements also define your team's psychological approach to teamwork. They are a written version of your team's thought system.

A team without Work Agreements is like a machine without an operator's manual. Teammates might function at acceptable levels for a while, but eventually, they will decline into separateness and egotistical self-interest.

A Work Agreement is a covenant, promise, or pledge that transforms dysfunctional and non-productive work behavior. It is not a ground rule. It is an emotionally mature promise based on collaboration and achieving customer satisfaction.

Emotionally mature and productive teammates create Work Agreements that sustain Right-Minded Teamwork because they have experienced the benefits of a unified team with shared interests and common goals.

In the book ***Reason, Ego & the Right-Minded Teamwork Myth**: The Philosophy and Process for Creating a Right-Minded Team that Works Together as One,* you will learn that you – the Decision-Maker – always follow either Reason or Ego.

Reason encourages you and your teammates to create Work Agreements because Reason knows they will help you achieve 100% customer satisfaction. Creating and following your Agreements indicates you and your team are in charge of and in control of your collective Right Mind.

Ego, on the other hand, does not want you to make those Agreements. Ego wants you to be a victim, blame others, or be a victimizer who attacks others.

Ego will never lead you to do no harm and work as one. Effective Work Agreements can only be created from your team's collective Right Mind, with Reason's gentle guidance.

When you make and follow these teamwork promises, you unite with each other, not Ego. You return to the forgiving Unified Circle of Right-Minded Thinking, where recovering from difficult teammate situations is intuitive and natural.

Creating Work Agreements

Since you have been in many teams, you know it is not a matter of if conflict will occur among teammates. It is a question of when.

For that reason, it is far better to have Work Agreements in place before disagreements happen. Your existing Work Agreements will serve to mitigate and even make positive use of those clashes when they occur. However, even if your team is already in conflict, it's still not and will never be too late to create and live team Work Agreements.

In the book ***How to Facilitate Team Work Agreements**: A Practical, 10-Step Process for Building a Right-Minded Team That Works as One*, you will learn the fundamental principles for creating and facilitating Work Agreements. These steps will ensure you move your teammates into their collective Right Minds, which guarantees they make practical, powerful Work Agreements.

Two Types of Work Agreements

Almost all teamwork issues can be resolved with Work Agreements.

There are two types of Agreements.

1. A **Process Work Agreement** describes who does what and which work methods they use.

2. A **Behavioral Work Agreement** describes how people will behave while they perform their tasks.

Process Agreements define work tasks in terms of roles, responsibilities, interfaces, or procedures.

Behavioral Agreements highlight, with transparency, the ways teammates bring to light, communicate, and resolve difficult performance issues or interpersonal conflicts.

Work Agreement Structure

A Work Agreement that is wholeheartedly agreed upon includes an **intention statement** that defines your team's choice followed by **clarifications or conditions for acceptance**.

Example:

Intention:
Each teammate will communicate their thoughts and feelings in appropriate ways.

Clarifications or Conditions:

- We follow the spirit and intent of our company values.
- If we believe another person is communicating inappropriately, we will call it to their attention in private.
- Even though this Agreement addresses inappropriate communication behaviors, we also agree to give positive teammate reinforcement when we see and hear excellent communication.

Real Team Work Agreements

Below you will find two real examples. The first one is a behavioral team Communication Work Agreement. The other is a process, Decision-Making Work Agreement.

I worked with these teams for a few years. They were phenomenally successful Agreements because teammates passionately created and actively lived them day in and day out.

Behavioral Agreement – Communication

Team Choice: Intention Statement

1. Each teammate will communicate in a respectful way.

Clarifications / Conditions for Acceptance:

A. We will use good communication techniques that include appropriate body language and tone of voice, plus suitable words.
B. If we see or hear disrespect or we hear an inappropriate behind-the-back conversation, we own it and need to step in.
C. If someone unintentionally shows disrespect, we will give them the benefit of the doubt, let them know, and create a new way to interact going forward.
D. We will actively support team decisions in word, deed, and energy; we will use our decision-making protocol agreement for key decisions.
E. We will be on time for meetings.
F. We will ask, "May I interrupt you?"
G. We will use observable facts during disagreements and decision-making, and we will acknowledge when we are using assumptions.
H. We will understand each other's roles, ask for help if we need it, share relevant information and if helpful, give constructive feedback in private.
I. If someone continues to break this agreement, we will tell them that we will invite a third party to help if there is continued disagreement. If that doesn't solve the issues, we will all go to a higher authority for support and resolution.

Process Agreement – Decision-Making Protocol
Team Choice: Intention Statement 1. We will go for consensus for all key team decisions, but our fallback will be that Maria [team leader] will decide if we cannot reach a consensus.
Conditions for Acceptance / Clarification A. Before entering a discussion, we'll agree on the decision-making method and fall back, plus when [date] a decision will be made. B. Before delving into a solution, we will create an opportunity or problem statement. C. At the beginning of our discussion, we will determine boundaries & givens (i.e., time sensitivity; cost, hassle, impact, 80% or 100% perfect decision, etc.). D. We provide a business case (appropriate justification) for our decision, including cost/benefit. E. During our conversations, we will advocate and inquire. We will not hold back. For instance, we will acknowledge assumptions and facts. F. To create the best solutions, we will also think about alternative ways to test our solution (Devil's Advocate). G. If we find ourselves at an impasse, we will call a "time out" to calm down or acquire more technical information. H. When a decision is made, we will accurately represent and support the decision. I. We do this Agreement because we want to improve teamwork and trust in one another. J. We will hold ourselves and others accountable for living the letter and the spirit of this Agreement; we will fine-tune it as necessary

With my guidance, it took this 10-person team about 4 hours to create these two Work Agreements. Use your imagination as to what they said to each other that made these successful agreements.

Onboarding New Teammates

When a new leader or teammate joins your team, it is vitally important to properly onboard them within their first week on the job. In a single short meeting where everyone attends, the onboarding is easily and effectively accomplished. Present all your RMT goals and Work Agreements along with why they were created. They ask you clarifying questions. Afterward, you ask them to accept the team's goals and actively live the team's Work Agreements.

How to Facilitate Team Work Agreements

The communication Work Agreement shown above is also used as a teaching aid in the book ***How to Facilitate Team Work Agreements****: A Practical, 10-Step Process for Building a Right-Minded Team That Works as One*.

Below you will find a summary of these ten steps. To apply them effectively, you will want to read and study the full process explained in the book. There, you will learn the detailed methodology I successfully applied with over 500 teams in seven different countries. I guarantee it will help your team create Work Agreements, too.

A Brief Narrative Summary of the 10 Steps.

Schedule a Team-Building Workshop

Let's start by assuming a team leader has decided to conduct a one-day Work Agreements workshop and has asked you to facilitate it. Here are the preparation and facilitation steps.

First Decide: In-Person or Virtual Workshop?

If you must conduct a virtual workshop, the same principles, concepts, and steps presented here still apply. Use a video software conferencing platform to ensure all participants can see each other and the virtual flip chart used for capturing your team Work Agreements.

However, if possible, **an in-person workshop is the superior choice** because teammates can see and feel each other's attitudes and behaviors.

Preparation Steps 1-3

Take these steps before the workshop:

1. Agree on the first teamwork topic to address, which will result in a Work Agreement.

2. Determine the topic's desired outcome.

3. Design an opening question to be asked to kick off the topic dialogue.

In **Step 1**, the team leader informs the facilitator what they want to achieve and why.

Often, some difficult situation has occurred that has precipitated the desire for this workshop. After you understand the leader's desired teamwork outcomes, you then interview all teammates to also understand what they want to achieve and why.

After the teammate interviews, you share the team's collective input with the leader, which results in selecting teamwork topics to address in the first workshop. In the book ***How to Facilitate Team Work Agreements****: A Practical, 10-Step Process for Building a Right-Minded Team That Works as One,* we use two outcomes as teaching examples: improving communication and team decision-making. The first is a behavioral issue, and the second is a work process issue.

In **Step 2**, an agenda is created that includes the desired outcomes.

In **Step 3**, an opening question is created for both issues: communication and decision-making. In the workshop, the facilitator asks those questions to launch a team discussion. Eventually, this discussion leads to one or more Work Agreements.

Facilitation Steps 4-10

4. When the time is right, ask the opening question for your topic.

5. Capture legitimate behavioral answers on a flipchart.

6. Write and propose an intention statement.

7. After a short dialogue, ask if teammates agree to live the intention.

8. Write clarifications and conditions for acceptance.

9. Create an interlocking accountability condition.

10. When everyone approves the Work Agreement, celebrate. Move to the next topic.

The Workshop

Imagine you are 10 minutes into your workshop. The team leader has welcomed everyone. All teammates have agreed to the desired outcomes, agenda, ground rules, and the day's logistics.

Before you ask your opening question, take five minutes to introduce the **Right Choice Model**. Your goal is to present the model in such a way that when you finish teaching it, all teammates declare,

> *Of course, we need to approach [our issue] in a Right-Minded, accountable way. Let's get started.*

Another option is the team leader could present the Right Choice Model by relating it to a current difficult team challenge.

Either way, after you present it and the team's collective "Decision-Maker" has made that commitment, it is the right time for you to ask the opening question.

To learn more about the Right Choice Model and how to apply it in your team, go to RightMindedTeamwork.com or your favorite book retailer, and pick up ***How to Apply the Right Choice Model:*** *Create a Right-Minded Team That Works as One*. Within the book, look for the section titled, "How to Present & Apply the Right Choice Model in Your Team." There, you will be given specific instructions on how to present the Right Choice Model successfully.

Asking the opening question officially starts an honest discussion on the first teamwork topic - **Step 4.** Here is a good opening question example: *If we communicated respectfully, what would you see or hear teammates say or do, or not say or do?*

Up to this point, you have been doing most of the talking. After asking the opening question, you move into listening, observing, and facilitating.

Now that the opening question has been asked, you listen to the team's discussion, which may last 30-60 minutes. All the while, you are capturing legitimate behavioral answers on a flipchart - **Step 5**.

In **Step 6,** while teammates continue to discuss their workshop topic, you think about and write an intention statement. The proposed statement should evolve from the team's list of answers. When the time is right, you suggest the intention statement. Here is an example: *Each teammate will communicate in a respectful way with each other and our customers.*

In **Step 7**, you ask teammates if they will agree to live the proposed intention. Most of the time, teammates agree. But they usually believe it needs more work. It is still a work in progress.

In **Step 8,** the team discusses their specific clarifications or conditions for acceptance of the intention statement. As teammates add and edit their conditions, you and the team leader periodically ask them, if they truly lived their Work-Agreement-in-progress, would they achieve their desired outcome? Most of the time, they will say yes. This "yes" motivates the team to continue making the "right" Agreement for this team.

Finally, **Step 9** calls for "interlocking accountability" within the Work Agreement - a vital step to encouraging the team to live their Agreements day in and day out. Fortunately, you will only need to create interlocking accountability once. It will apply to all Work Agreements.

For a real-world example of interlocking accountability, flip back a few pages to the section "Real Team Work Agreements" and look at the final condition in the behavioral Communication Agreement.

In **Step 10**, every teammate publicly commits to hold themselves and others accountable for upholding the team Work Agreement. At this point, everyone should genuinely believe the Agreement will help the team achieve its goals.

It's important to note that it's not unusual for people to break their Work Agreements after the workshop. Often, this breach is just an honest mistake or a habit not yet transformed. However, if a teammate continues to break a Work Agreement, the team should have an agreed-upon condition [step 9's interlocking accountability] that clarifies how they will confront one another.

To Learn More…

For more Work Agreement examples, check out the **RMT Implementation Plan – 4 Actual Examples** in the Resources section of this book.

5 Elements of Right-Minded TEAMWORK

Element #4
Team Operating System: Make Yours Effective

A Right-Minded Teamwork Team Operating System is a 90-day, continuous improvement plan that ensures your team stays focused on achieving 100% customer satisfaction.

Your Team Operating System organizes your team processes and procedures. There are six components.

Six Steps Team Operating System

1. Enterprise Vision & Strategy

The senior leadership team creates a high-level vision and strategy. Every team within the organization is accountable for implementing their part.

2. Team Mission & Goals

Once teammates understand their team's responsibility and accountability to the enterprise's vision and strategy, they create a team mission, business goals, and psychological goals.

The team's mission and goals ensure the team focuses its energy and resources on achieving 100% customer satisfaction.

3. Team Assessment

With clear direction, the team conducts the ***Team Performance Factor Assessment*** to determine what the team needs to start, stop, or continue doing to achieve its mission and goals. The team assessment identifies improvement opportunities.

This review ensures the team stays focused and on track. This team assessment is re-administered every quarter, and adjustments are made accordingly.

See a more detailed description of the *Team Performance Factor Assessment* at the end of this section.

4. Team Choices

In this segment, teams determine their two to three critical-few projects, deliverables, or initiatives to achieve over the next 90 days.

These actions will improve these Team Performance Factors:

- Financial Goals
- Product or Service Quality
- Work Efficiency
- Teammate Relationships

They also choose how they will make progress toward those projects or goals, using one or more of RMT's three strategies:

- Create process Work Agreements
- Create behavioral Work Agreements
- Implement an improvement project

See a more detailed description of each of these three strategies below in *Three Team Improvement Strategies*.

5. Team Business Plan

All team choices, especially the two to three critical-few projects, are captured in a Team Business Plan, a document used to guide and track the team's efforts over the next 90 days (and every quarter after that).

6. Report of Improvement

Every 90 days, the team conducts another team assessment that calculates actual performance improvement.

Based on assessment results, a Report of Improvement is created and presented to the team's sponsor or supervisor. In the improvement report, the team also captures key lessons learned as well as their best and worst practices.

If your organization has an **RMT Team Management System** [TMS], your quarterly Report of Improvement and lessons learned are given to the TMS Leadership Team for company tabulation and knowledge sharing.

Next, the team leader reinforces clarity by confirming its mission and goals align with company-driven objectives. If the team's objectives align with the company's objectives, the team repeats the continuous improvement system by examining Team Performance Factor Assessment results, identifying opportunities, and taking action on their findings.

To Learn More…

Go to the Resources section of this book and find **RMT Implementation Plan – 4 Actual Examples**. Examples 2, 3, and 4 to see three real Team Business Plan examples.

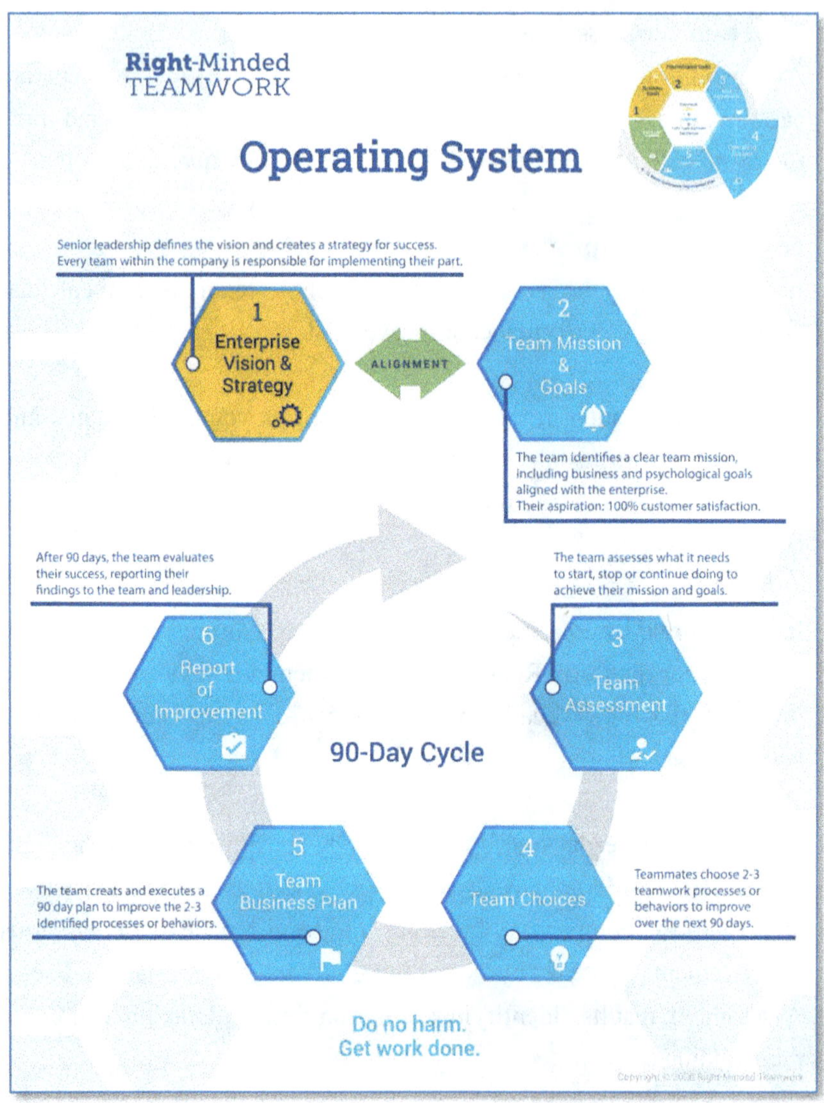
Right-Minded
TEAMWORK
Operating System
Senior leadership defines the vision and creates a strategy for success.
Every team within the company is responsible for implementing their part.
1
Enterprise Vision & Strategy
ALIGNMENT
2
Team Mission & Goals
The team identifies a clear team mission, including business and psychological goals aligned with the enterprise.
Their aspiration: 100% customer satisfaction.
After 90 days, the team evaluates their success, reporting their findings to the team and leadership.
The team assesses what it needs to start, stop or continue doing to achieve their mission and goals.
6
Report of Improvement
3
Team Assessment
90-Day Cycle
5
Team Business Plan
4
Team Choices
The team creats and executes a 90 day plan to improve the 2-3 identified processes or behaviors.
Teammates choose 2-3 teamwork processes or behaviors to improve over the next 90 days.
Do no harm.
Get work done.

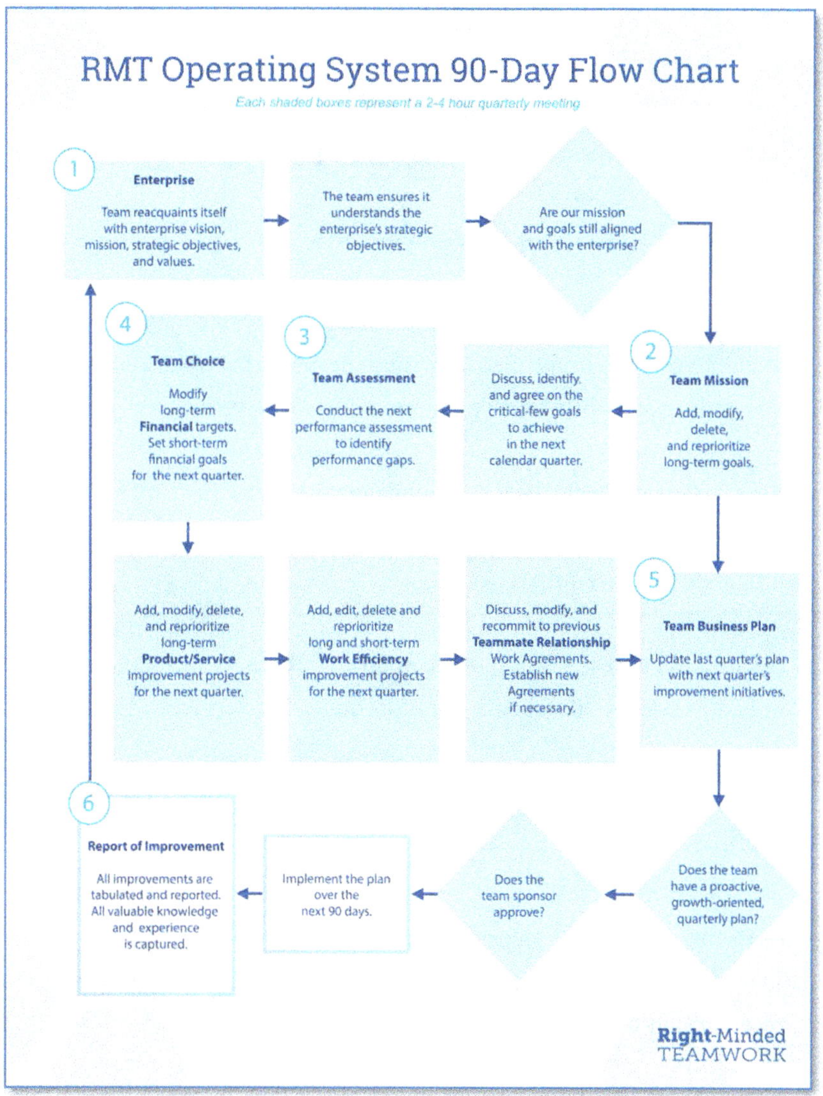
RMT Operating System 90-Day Flow Chart
Each shaded boxes represent a 2-4 hour quarterly meeting
1
Enterprise
Team reacquaints itself with enterprise vision, mission, strategic objectives, and values.
The team ensures it understands the enterprise's strategic objectives.
Are our mission and goals still aligned with the enterprise?
2
Team Mission
Add, modify, delete, and reprioritize long-term goals.
Discuss, identify, and agree on the critical-few goals to achieve in the next calendar quarter.
3
Team Assessment
Conduct the next performance assessment to identify performance gaps.
4
Team Choice
Modify long-term Financial targets. Set short-term financial goals for the next quarter.
Add, modify, delete, and reprioritize long-term Product/Service improvement projects for the next quarter.
Add, edit, delete and reprioritize long and short-term Work Efficiency improvement projects for the next quarter.
Discuss, modify, and recommit to previous Teammate Relationship Work Agreements. Establish new Agreements if necessary.
5
Team Business Plan
Update last quarter's plan with next quarter's improvement initiatives.
Does the team have a proactive, growth-oriented, quarterly plan?
Does the team sponsor approve?
Implement the plan over the next 90 days.
6
Report of Improvement
All improvements are tabulated and reported. All valuable knowledge and experience is captured.
Right-Minded TEAMWORK

Three Team Improvement Strategies

As a team, teammates choose one or more of these strategies to help them make progress toward achieving projects or goals.

1. Create Process Work Agreements.

These Agreements usually improve ineffective processes and procedures. They may also clarify important teamwork topics, like roles and responsibilities or team meeting effectiveness.

The Agreements are discussed and agreed upon in a team meeting. Teammates follow these Agreements and, as a result, see an immediate positive impact.

Outcome: Process Work Agreements reduce workload, eliminate duplication, and add value to team products and services.

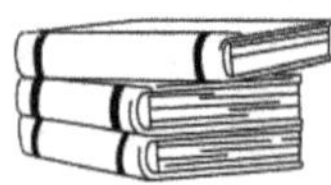

To Learn More…

Go to the Resources section below and find **RMT Implementation Plan – 4 Actual Examples**. Read in Example #3 – International Project Team how this team's…

> ***Process** Work Agreement saved them USD $10,000 per week in labor costs.*

2. Create Behavioral Work Agreements.

These Agreements improve team relationships in essential areas such as increasing trust and respect or resolving workplace conflicts.

These Agreements are also created in a team meeting. Often, team members feel optimistic that their collective Agreements will benefit everyone. Teammates immediately follow these Agreements, though it usually takes a few weeks to a month of practice before the team begins to see positive results and improved team relationships.

Outcome: Behavioral Work Agreements improve teammate trust, increase risk-taking, and create team loyalty and accountability.

To Learn More…

Go to the Resources section below and find **RMT Implementation Plan – 4 Actual Examples**. Read in Example #2 – Field Support Team how this team's…

> ***Behavioral*** *Work Agreement increased their trust in one another by 78%.*

3. Implement an Improvement Project.

An improvement project is also discussed and agreed upon in a team meeting, but it is more complicated than a Work Agreement.

A team Improvement Project will:

- Take a group of two or more teammates to resolve
- Need a thorough analysis before making a final decision
- Require two to 12 weeks to address and analyze thoroughly
- Use objective data like the number of errors, cost per error, and categorization of mistakes (sorted by type and how urgently the error needs fixing)

Improvement Project examples:

- Improve work scheduling efficiency
- Improve customer and supplier communication
- Reduce product and service mistakes
- Improve the decision-making process and quality
- Improve weak or inefficient pass-offs between customer and supplier teams
- Fix the problem of missed customer deliveries due to inadequate communication between internal departments

To Learn More…

Go to the Resources section below and find **RMT Implementation Plan – 4 Actual Examples**. Read in Example #1 – Nuclear Power Generating Plant how the senior leadership team's…

> ***Improvement Project**, a site-wide plan they named a 100-day Behavioral Outage, positively changed the organization's culture.*

Creating Your Team Operating System

RMT's Team Operating System is, as its name states, a systematic process. It always works when you follow it.

Once your team completes the first two 90-day iterations, the process will gain speed and momentum, making it much faster than the first time. Eventually, you will become so adept at the steps included in your 90-day iterations that they will become second nature.

In summary, the steps are:

- Using the *Team Performance Factor Assessment*, choose two to three improvement opportunities for the next 90 days.
- Create effective solutions.
- Implement those solutions for the next 90 days.
- Ensure those solutions are self-sustaining.
- Repeat the process every 90 days.

After studying the *Team Performance Factors Assessment* below, you might think it asks too much or that it is too hard. Please, put that thought aside for a little while.

Remember, *you do not have to fix all parts* of your Operating System at once. You must only choose the most critical improvement opportunities to improve *now*. When you look at the performance factors, you will see a carefully planned process that *will strengthen* your current operating system.

Before we discuss the performance factors, let's take a moment to learn how Right-Minded teams ***make good decisions***.

Decision-Making Work Agreement

Every Right-Minded team has a Decision-Making Work Agreement that clearly defines how decisions are made and who makes them. Creating an agreement and putting it into your team's Operating System's Business Plan as a team Work Agreement makes good business sense.

If you do not currently have a team Decision-Making agreement or you have not updated it recently, I highly recommend you do that as soon as it is practical. Incidentally, Decision-Making is #18 in the *Team Performance Factor Assessment.*

Range of Decision-Making Options

There is no one right way to construct your Decision-Making Agreement, but here are some guidelines and definitions that will help. Below are four decision-making options you can use.

1. Command

In this option, the leader decides and announces their decision to teammates. This option is suitable for emergencies and inconsequential types of decisions. When the leader announces their choice, teammates will happily abide by the leader's decision.

2. Consult

The leader gathers information and recommendations in small group meetings or with others outside the team in this decision-making option. As with the command option, teammates will abide by their decision when the leader announces their choice.

3. Consensus

In this option, the team desires to reach a consensus. Everyone has equal authority to persuade and advocate for what they believe to be the best decision.

Consensus does not mean that everyone agrees. What it means, in the end, is that everyone will **actively support** the decision in word and deed even if they did not get everything they wanted.

Fall-Back: *before the team discusses an issue*, the team will create a fall-back decision-making option to use if the team cannot reach a consensus.

For example, you might agree to take a vote and the decision with the most votes wins. Or you could default to a Subject Matter Expert or the team leader who will make the final decision.

There is no perfect Fall-Back. But it is **highly recommended** that you agree upon the Fall Back decision method ***before*** discussing the problem that needs a decision.

4. Delegation

In this option, the leader gives the team or a subgroup the authority to decide ***if*** they adhere to specific guidelines and boundaries such as cost and time.

When the group announces their choice, the leader and teammates will abide by the group's decision.

Decision-Making Guidelines

Use some or all of these guidelines in your team's Decision-Making Work Agreement.

- An effective Decision-Making Work Agreement requires facilitating the team through two distinctively different activities.

  First, **define the problem** and,

  Secondly, **solve the problem**.

  Go to the Resources section below and find **RMT Implementation Plan – 4 Actual Examples**. In Example #3 – International Project Team, this team created and used *"The Problem is"* statements method to frame their problem before offering solutions. It was a very successful strategy.

- For the more important decisions, always allow enough time to discuss the issue thoroughly to ensure you properly define the problem and remind teammates of your RMT motto – **None of us is as smart as all of us**.

- It's best to avoid debates, and please announce in advance if you are deciding to play a devil's advocate role.

- It's also best not to *"immediately"* settle for majority rule, compromises, or trade-offs; always go into every discussion by looking for a win/win solution.

- Once you make the decision, everyone on the team agrees to actively support it.

- It's best not to interpret a teammate's silence as support. For some decisions, ask each person to state out loud why they support the decision.

- Decide what the group will tell others outside the team about the decision. If necessary, script a standard communication that all agree to follow without spin or innuendo.

What is Consensus?

Consensus is not the same as 100% agreement. It does mean that all teammates agree to *actively support the team's decision*, even though it might not be their personal choice.

How do you know you have reached a consensus?

When each teammate can say with confidence:

- My personal views and ideas have been listened to and seriously considered.
- I have openly listened to and seriously considered the ideas and views of every other team member.
- Whether or not this decision would have been my choice, I will actively support it and work towards its implementation and success.

Here's an actual Decision-Making Work Agreement.

In the book, ***How to Facilitate Team Work Agreements****: A Practical, 10-Step Process for Building a Right-Minded Team That Works as One*, you will find two examples.

The first one is a behavioral Communication Agreement, and the other is the **Decision-Making Work Agreement** below.

I worked with this team for a few years. They were phenomenally successful Agreements because teammates passionately created and actively lived them day in and day out.

Process Agreement – Decision-Making Protocol
Team Choice: Intention Statement 1. We will go for consensus for all key team decisions, but our fallback will be that Maria [team leader] will decide if we cannot reach a consensus.
Conditions for Acceptance / Clarification A. Before entering a discussion, we'll agree on the decision-making method and fall back, plus when [date] a decision will be made. B. Before delving into a solution, we will create an opportunity or problem statement. C. At the beginning of our discussion, we will determine boundaries & givens (i.e., time sensitivity; cost, hassle, impact, 80% or 100% perfect decision, etc.). D. We provide a business case (appropriate justification) for our decision, including cost/benefit. E. During our conversations, we will advocate and inquire. We will not hold back. For instance, we will acknowledge assumptions and facts. F. To create the best solutions, we will also think about alternative ways to test our solution (Devil's Advocate). G. If we find ourselves at an impasse, we will call a "time out" to calm down or acquire more technical information. H. When a decision is made, we will accurately represent and support the decision. I. We do this Agreement because we want to improve teamwork and trust in one another. J. We will hold ourselves and others accountable for living the letter and the spirit of this Agreement; we will fine-tune it as necessary

Team Performance Factor Assessment

The Team Operating System is a six-step, 90-day, continuous improvement operating system that organizes your team functions to increase the likelihood of achieving customer satisfaction.

The system includes the *Team Performance Factor Assessment*, which you will use to help teammates identify two to three improvement opportunities every 90 days.

The 25 performance factors in this assessment are perfectly aligned with and thus effectively measure the six steps of your operating system. They measure all aspects of Right-Minded Teamwork.

To download a reusable copy of this assessment to distribute to your teammates, go to RightMindedTeamwork.com, and search for this book's companion ***Reusable Resources & Templates***.

Below is an example of the first five questions in that document.

Team Performance Factor Assessment

Team Leader: ______________ Assessment Date: ______________

Teammate: ______________ Team Facilitator: ______________

Performance Factor	Comments about the Current State	Address This Quarter	Address Next Quarter	Address After 6 months
Step 1 – Enterprise				
1. The enterprise's vision, strategy, and strategic objectives are clear, understandable, and agreeable to our team.				
2. The enterprise's values are clearly stated and embraced by our team. We believe our psychological goals and our work agreements align with them.				
3. Our team sponsor's strategic objectives are clear, understood, and aligned with those of the enterprise.				
4. Our team understands its responsibility for achieving our sponsor's objectives.				
5. Senior leadership, our team sponsor, and our team members communicate openly to ensure our team is doing its part to fulfill the enterprise's strategic plan.				

Instructions

1. Each teammate reviews the 25 **Team Performance Factors**.

2. Each teammate places a checkmark next to the 2 to 3 performance factors they believe the team should address in the upcoming 90 days.

3. Give teammates a few days to complete their assessment. Teammates return their completed assessment to the team leader or facilitator.

4. All assessments are tallied and distributed to all team members before the next 90-day RMT team-building workshop.

5. Right-Minded Teamwork advocates that all teams meet every 90 days to conduct a real-world and performance-focused team-building workshop.

   In this workshop, teammates will review their *Team Performance Factor Assessment* results and choose the 2 to 3 performance factors the team will improve during the upcoming 90 days.

   The team repeats this process every 90 days.

Team Performance Factor Assessment

Step 1 – Enterprise Vision & Strategy

1. The enterprise's vision, strategy, and strategic objectives are clear, understandable, and agreeable to our team.
2. The enterprise's values are clearly stated and embraced by our team. We believe our psychological goals and our work agreements align with them.
3. Our team sponsor's strategic objectives are clear, understood, and aligned with those of the enterprise.
4. Our team understands its responsibility for achieving our sponsor's objectives.
5. Senior leadership, our team sponsor, and our team members communicate openly to ensure our team is doing its part to fulfill the enterprise's strategic plan.

Step 2 – Team Mission & Goals

6. Our team has a team mission and business and psychological goals that align with our sponsor's objectives.
7. All our teammates actively support our team's mission and goals.

Step 3 – Team Assessment

8. Our team follows a holistic team assessment process to evaluate business processes and teamwork relationships and identify improvements needed to achieve our team's mission and goals.
9. The team has a clear set of 90-day goals as well as potential long-term objectives.
10. Our team is consistently following a short and long-term team development plan, like Right-Minded Teamwork.

Step 4 – Team Choices

11. **Our Financial Performance** – Our team has a budget or P&L.
12. Each team member understands their role in the team's financial performance.

13. **Our Product/Service Quality** – Each team member understands our team's deliverables and can adequately explain the features and benefits to anyone.
14. Our team has a process in place for continually improving our team's product and service offerings.

15. **Our Work Process Efficiencies** – Every teammate understands, accepts, and supports our team's operating systems and reporting responsibilities.
16. Our team has established effective and efficient work processes that will achieve our mission and business goals.
17. All teammates are clear about their roles, responsibilities, and accountability.
18. All teammates understand, accept, and support the team's decision-making process and protocols.
19. Our team meetings are practical and efficient. We update our Team Business Plan in team meetings, which tracks actual team performance and lessons learned.

20. **Our Team Relationships** - Each team member holds themselves and others accountable for following our team's psychological goals, our company values, and team Work Agreements.
21. Each team member and the team's sponsor agree to do what they can to improve team unity, collaboration, and alignment.

Step 5 – Team Business Plan

22. Our team captures all Agreements, projects, action items, and improvement ideas in a Business Plan that is updated minimally every calendar quarter.

Step 6 – Report Improvement; Capture Knowledge

23. Every 90 days, our team conducts another team assessment that calculates and reports our actual performance improvement while also recognizing and acknowledging individual and group efforts. The assessment report is presented to our team's sponsor.
24. Additionally, the report includes our critical lessons learned and the best and worst practices from the previous quarter. If the enterprise has a central depository for lessons learned, the report is forwarded to that department.
25. Finally, our team leader ensures that our team's mission and goals align with our sponsor's objectives.

    Presuming they are, our team repeats the 90-day continuous improvement process, beginning with the Team Performance Factor Assessment.

Note: To see a real, although abbreviated version of how a team used Performance Factors, go to the Resources section at the end of this book and find ***Example #2: Field Support Team.***

5 Elements of Right-Minded TEAMWORK

Element #5
Right-Minded Teammates: Strengthen Performance

As a teammate, Right-Minded Teamwork gives you a toolbox full of tools to improve your work experience.

Are you seeking satisfied customers? Do you want to work with collaborative and enjoyable teammates? Do you wish you were part of a team where trust and respect thrive, conflicts are mutually resolved, and teammates support each other in growing their skills and talents?

Creating and sustaining Right-Minded Teamwork delivers all these results and more.

Right-Minded Teamwork for Individuals

Working in a Right-Minded team strengthens your ability to be mindful, present, and aware at an individual level.

Rather than waking up each morning in a panic, dreading what the day may bring, you wake up feeling your work is important and valuable. Your contributions matter. Knowing this brings you happiness and joy. Your deep satisfaction helps you greet the day ahead.

When you go to sleep each evening, that feeling of fulfillment calms your mind. You are full of gratitude and honored to work with such an incredible team. You are surrounded by teammates who, each day, demonstrate ***your team's*** Right-Minded attitudes and behaviors.

In RMT's book ***Reason, Ego & the Right-Minded Teamwork Myth**: The Philosophy and Process for Creating a Right-Minded Team that Works Together as One*, you learned that you – the Decision-Maker – follow either Reason or Ego.

Reason encourages you to strengthen your ability to be mindful because Reason knows that by doing so, you will succeed in doing your part to help your team achieve 100% customer satisfaction.

You also learned that you act like a victim or victimizer when you follow Ego, which only hurts you and your team's performance.

Because you have consciously chosen to follow Reason, it is much easier for you to recover from any difficult team situation because you have, at that moment, restored your Right Mind to Reason.

You merely **do no harm** while you **work as one**.

Aspiring to Be a Right-Minded Teammate

Every teammate brings two talents to their team: **technical skill** and **personal attitude**.

RMT acknowledges that individuals possess a wide range of technical skills. For example, one teammate could possess strong computer skills while another has exceptional customer service skills. It is not practical to ask the customer service teammate to learn how to fix computers; RMT advocates putting teammates in jobs that best suit their technical skills.

Regardless of their specific roles, Right-Minded Teammates put effort into improving their skills. They also consciously embrace Right-Minded attitudes throughout their workday, focusing their attention on doing the right things the right way, with the right attitude.

When things go wrong, or they realize they are doing the right things the wrong way or with the wrong attitude, Right-Minded Teammates self-adjust their attitude and behavior, usually through a **moment of Reason.**

They strive to always **do no harm** and **work as one**, actively living the two cornerstone principles of Right-Minded Teamwork.

Combining Skills & Right-Minded Attitudes

One of the best available tools for building teamwork is the book ***Right-Minded Teamwork**: 9 Right Choices for Building a Team That Works as One.*

Of the nine choices, the seventh choice is:

> *Mistakes happen. Correct them; don't punish people.*

In this choice, when mistakes occur, teammates are asked to trust Reason above Ego. Too often, our instinctual reaction is to criticize, point fingers, or deny responsibility.

> *But if teams are to work as one, the mistake of one is also the mistake of the whole team.*

Rather than blaming the person who made a mistake, Reason encourages you to rise above the battleground to a place in your mind that is strictly solution-focused, not blame-based.

Despite your differences and their inadvertent error, Reason knows you and your teammate have the same goal. The only way forward is to accept what has happened, forgive all involved, and make the necessary adjustments to prevent it from happening again. Focusing on solutions that move you towards that goal allows you to rise above your differences and work together. Ultimately, this shift helps strengthen individual and team performance.

For example, if a teammate skilled with computers spots a mistake made by a customer service teammate, instead of reacting with anger or blaming the customer service expert, the computer expert could extend an offer to help.

If treated with empathy and understanding, how would the customer service expert respond? Rather than feeling a need to shut down or become defensive, the customer service expert would likely be grateful, if a bit surprised, to receive a genuine offer of support. Together, they could find a way to correct the error and recover.

In this example, the Right-Minded attitude of correcting mistakes and the Right-Minded skill of proper communication brought the situation to an amicable, productive close.

The 10 Characteristics of Right-Minded Teammates

Right-Minded Teammates have diverse backgrounds, and vastly different experiences, and display a wide range of skills. No two are alike. Still, there are certain characteristics all Right-Minded Teammates share.

These characteristics align the teammate's authentic self with the RMT motto of *Do no harm and work as one*. They are:

1. Trust
2. Honesty
3. Tolerance
4. Gentleness
5. Joy
6. Defenselessness
7. Generosity
8. Patience
9. Open-mindedness
10. Faithfulness

When you help your team create and live team Work Agreements, they will be well on their way to living these characteristics.

How does the Right-Minded Teammate live these characteristics?

They do two things when difficult situations occur.

First, they remind themselves of their commitment to *thinking* in a do-no-harm way. Second, they choose to demonstrate do-no-harm *behaviors* that align with their Right-Minded attitudes, such as finding solutions to challenging situations.

It is not always easy to do these two things, but it is always that simple.

To encourage your team to embrace and live these Right-Minded characteristics, check out these two RMT books:

7 Mindfulness Training Lessons: *Improve Teammates' Ability to Work as One with Right-Minded Thinking* will teach you how to apply RMT's seven, powerful thinking lessons to encourage Right-Minded, unified teamwork.

How to Apply the Right Choice Model: *Create a Right-Minded Team That Works as One* teaches you how to transform a disappointed team customer into a 100% satisfied customer by making Right-Minded choices, all of which align with the above list of characteristics.

For now, though, let's take a closer look at each of these 10, Right-Minded Teammate characteristics.

1. Trust

Trust is the foundational characteristic for teammates who desire to create and sustain Right-Minded Teamwork. Right-Minded Teammates trust one another because their own past experience has taught them that, in all situations, a forgiving attitude creates safety for teammates to collaborate and resolve difficulties.

2. Honesty

For the Right-Minded Teammate, honesty means more than just telling the truth. It refers to consistency in thought and deed. An honest, Right-Minded Teammate is consistently looking within and striving to align thoughts, words, and behaviors with the team's psychological goals and forgiving values. This kind of honesty is essential to creating and sustaining Right-Minded Teamwork.

3. Tolerance

Judgment is the opposite of forgiveness; it implies a lack of trust. Tolerance indicates non-judgment. Tolerant teammates do not judge one another because they know that though they are not the same, all Right-Minded Teammates are equal. Their tolerance creates space for the wisdom of diversity to surface, and their equality allows them to work together as one.

4. Gentleness

Right-Minded Teammates believe that gentleness is the only sane response to challenging situations and circumstances. Whereas harshness and judgment close doors, gentleness opens them. With gentleness, it is easy for teammates to do no harm as they work as one – with teammates and customers alike.

5. Joy

Joy is the inevitable result of Right-Minded teammates who are gentle and non-judgmental. Fear is impossible for those who are gentle, especially during challenging situations. Joy comes from gentleness, tolerance, honesty, and forgiveness.

6. Defenselessness

Right-Minded Teammates understand that defenses are foolish, judgmental attitudes and behaviors that prevent the team from finding solutions to difficult situations. When teammates summon the courage to forgive and trust themselves and to look honestly at their wrong-minded defenses without judgment, they can lay those debilitating arguments gently aside, creating the proper conditions for honestly doing no harm and working as one.

7. Generosity

Right-Minded Teammates honestly and humbly give all they know to help their team create Right-Minded Teamwork and achieve 100% customer satisfaction. The world teaches that if you give something away, you lose it, but Right-Minded Teammates realize that to give *is* to receive. They eagerly participate with their teammates to create solutions to solve challenging situations, bringing joy and satisfaction to the team through their gentle generosity.

8. Patience

Teammates who know Right-Minded Teamwork is the outcome they want can easily afford to wait without concern. Because their goal is to be tolerant and gentle with their teammates, patience comes naturally. The highest desire is to work as one.

9. Open-Mindedness

Judgment, or wrong-mindedness, closes teammates' minds, creating resistance to Right-Minded Teamwork. To ensure they do no harm while working as one, Right-Minded Teammates embrace open-mindedness, also known as Right-Mindedness.

10. Faithfulness

Faithfulness describes a teammate's trust in their team's version of Right-Minded Teamwork. When a teammate is faithful, they effortlessly and wholeheartedly believe in Right-Minded Teamwork. They *want* to do no harm and work as one. They know none of us is as smart as all of us. When applied during challenging circumstances, their faithfulness inevitably leads the team to happy outcomes.

Two Methods for Strengthening Individual Performance

To improve individual performance within your team, you can:

1. Conduct a Right-Minded Teammate development workshop.
2. Implement one-on-one coaching or training.

Though either the workshop or individual training may come first in RMT's 5 Elements Implementation Plan, presented earlier in this book, it is usually best to address teammate development after teammates are on board with the team's psychological goals and Work Agreements.

Conduct a Right-Minded Teammate Development Workshop

To improve team performance, all teammates participate in a training workshop designed to improve a specific work skill or interpersonal talent.

Examples of work skill improvements include:

- Boosting team meeting effectiveness through facilitation skills training
- Implementing process improvement training, like Lean Six Sigma
- Using strategic planning exercises like the Balanced Performance Scorecard
- Improving team problem-solving and decision-making through Kepner Tregoe training

Examples of interpersonal talent improvements include:

- Clarifying teammate roles and responsibilities using RMT's Defining Teammate Roles and Responsibilities Exercise Using These Four Questions
- Improving individual effectiveness using the 7 Habits of Highly Effective People
- Learning about teammate personalities with tools like the Birkman method or RMT's About Me & My Preferences Team-Building Exercise
- Training teammates how to be assertive, not aggressive or passive, in their communications
- Increasing teammate trust by participating in a Speed of Trust training program or taking part in RMT's Trust Dialogue Team-Building Exercise

The three RMT Exercises above can be found in the Resources section of this book. You can also receive a downloadable copy of these exercises by going to RightMindedTeamwork.com and searching for this book's companion *Reusable Resources & Templates*.

The first step for implementing an improvement workshop is for teammates to brainstorm a list of development ideas.

Next, they pick a development topic. Then the team leader makes arrangements for the training workshop to occur.

Successful teams conduct at least one team development workshop per year.

Implement Individual Coaching & Training

When teammates brainstorm development ideas, it's natural for a Right-Minded Teammate to identify individual skills or talents they would like to improve.

Examples include:

- Learning a new software program or how to operate a new piece of equipment
- Studying for and obtaining a technical certification
- Attending a management or leadership training program
- Learning negotiation, mediation, or crisis management skills
- Improving the ability to communicate with difficult or angry people effectively

Since most work teams already conduct annual individual performance management assessments, RMT recommends each teammate record at least one personal development goal per year in their performance management program.

An individual development goal might be any of the above examples; however, RMT advocates all Right-Minded teammates to include developing Right-Minded Thinking as one of their goals.

Onboarding New Teammates

When a new leader or teammate joins your team, it is vitally important to properly onboard them within their first week on the job. In a single short meeting where everyone attends, the onboarding is easily and effectively accomplished. Present all your RMT goals and Work Agreements along with why they were created. They ask you clarifying questions. Afterward, you ask them to accept the team's goals and actively live the team's Work Agreements.

Right-Minded Teamwork Thinking

Right-Minded Thinking can be developed in many ways. One way to help teammates embrace Right-Minded Teamwork Thinking is through RMT's 7 Mindfulness Training Lessons.

In every circumstance, and especially during difficult team situations, Right-Minded Teammates seek Reason's Right-Minded way of thinking and behaving. Right-Minded Teammates use these 7 Lessons to ensure they always take Right-Minded action and consistently move in a positive direction.

These mindfulness lessons can be summed up in one sentence, with special emphasis on just three words:

> *Right-Minded Teammates* ***accept, forgive,*** *and* ***adjust*** *their thinking and work behavior.*

Mindfulness is your conscious ability to monitor your thoughts in the present and to calmly acknowledge and accept your thoughts, feelings, and behaviors as well as those of others.

When you practice mindfulness, it is easy to follow Reason's Right-Minded attitudes and behaviors because your choices are not reactive. You are simply aware of your thoughts and feelings. No matter what they are, you accept them. Then, you choose to follow Reason.

When you practice mindfulness, you demonstrate Right-Minded Teamwork behaviors. Even in crisis, you make mindful, intentional choices that align with your Work Agreements and team goals.

Applying the 7 Mindfulness Training Lessons is an easy way to consciously embrace Right-Minded attitudes throughout your workday.

7 Mindfulness Lessons of Right-Minded Teamwork Thinking

1. I am not upset about this team situation for the reason I think.
2. I **Accept** and own my part in this situation.
3. It's impossible for my thoughts about this situation to be neutral.
4. I **Forgive** others and myself.
5. I will transform the effects of this difficult team situation.
6. I **Adjust** my thinking and behavior.
7. I see every difficult team situation as a learning opportunity.

When individual teammates intentionally develop their Right-Minded Thinking skills and apply these lessons to mindfully navigate tricky team situations, Right-Minded Teamwork naturally follows. It becomes easy to **do no harm** while you **work as one.**

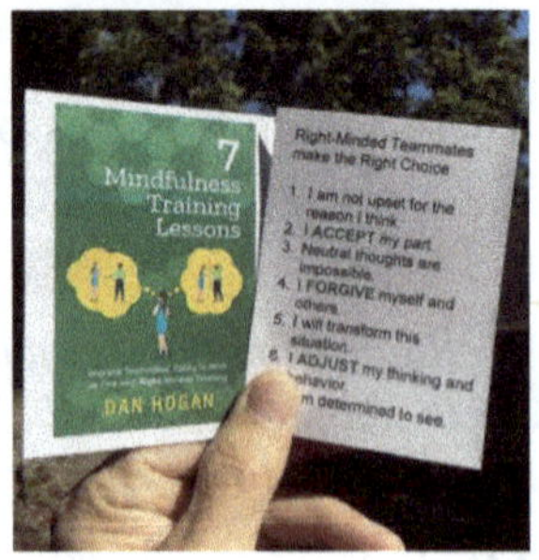

The End.
Your New Beginning.

When all 5 Elements of Right-Minded Teamwork's core framework are fully released into your team's operating system, you have established the proper condition for your new beginning towards successfully achieving Right-Minded Teamwork.

Ask Your Team to Imagine…

You are now thinking and behaving in a Right-Minded way. You are self-aware and focused on achieving your **team's business** and **psychological goals**. You consistently strive for **100% customer satisfaction**, and you always aim to **do no harm** while **working as one**.

To guide your steps, you have purposeful team **Work Agreements** describing your team's thought system. You get work done by leveraging your **Team Operating System**, identifying the critical few, focusing on solutions, and making true improvements.

As Right-Minded Teammates, you **willfully follow Reason**, behaving mindfully and positively in navigating difficult team situations. You have risen far above Ego's battleground to joyfully engage with one another in your work classroom, learning and growing every day. Happily, you find yourselves living more and more often in the **Unified Circle of Right-Minded Teamwork Thinking.**

Your New Beginning as a Right-Minded Teamwork Facilitator

Now that you understand each of RMT's 5 Elements and how they will benefit your client team, you are ready to implement RMT. Remember, even though there is no right way to implement RMT, the three-workshop Implementation Plan presented earlier in these pages will always work.

So, conduct the first workshop. Help teammates live their new team Work Agreements for a month or two and then conduct the second workshop. Trust the process. Keep them moving forward.

When they finish the third teammate development workshop, they will begin following their customized 90-day team operating plan. Every quarter, they will measure their progress and success. Each time, they will reinforce the value of RMT in their team.

Don't Forget!

As you begin your journey as a Right-Minded Teamwork facilitator, don't forget: good facilitation does not just happen on its own. You must practice and learn.

To bring your client teams together, you need guidance from proven, real-world methods, such as Right-Minded Teamwork. Moreover, you need to encourage your teammates to sincerely want to receive and follow this guidance, or the powerful teachings will be meaningless. Good teamwork must be a collaborative venture of commitment and growth.

Say to them,

> *If you want better teamwork, Right-Minded Teamwork can show you how to get there and what to do, but only with your help. Together with your teammates, you must believe that you have what it takes. With that conviction and Reason's guidance, you will collectively create and sustain Right-Minded Teamwork.*
>
> *Now, go and create Right-Minded Teamwork for yourself and your team, and know that* ***you are making the world better for everyone, everywhere, forever****.*

The End

Thanks for reading our Right-Minded Teamwork book. If you enjoyed it, wouldn't you please take a moment to leave a review at your favorite retailer or RightMindedTeamwork.com?

Also, in a few pages, you will find something beneficial: a ***Glossary of Right-Minded Teamwork Terms and Resources.***

And finally, on behalf of Reason and all the Right-Minded Teammate Decision-Makers and facilitators, we extend our best wishes to you and your teammates as they create another ***Right-Minded Team that Works Together as One***.

About the Author

The idea of "developing people and teams that work" began as a company statement for organizational consulting firm Lord & Hogan LLC, founded in 1990. Leveraging his personable but results-oriented consulting style, founder **Dan Hogan** devoted his career to transforming dysfunctional work relationships into positive, supportive bonds.

But over the course of his 40-year career, something shifted.

Through his work as an organizational development coach, performance consultant, and Certified Master Facilitator, the mission of Lord & Hogan also became Dan's own.

Better Work Relationships = Stronger, More Productive Teams

As a consultant and facilitator, Dan advocated for the individuals and managed teams he served. He emphasized the equal importance of strong team member relationships and solid business systems and processes to overall business success. His efforts spoke for themselves as his clients began to notice results.

With Dan's guidance, teams were more productive almost overnight. There were fewer day-to-day interpersonal issues. Project management efforts were finally back on track. Teams were achieving their goals.

After being stuck for so long, these teams were moving forward… smoothly. As one client said, "Dan has the unique ability to hear the confusion and bring clarity. He has helped me, our team, and our organization to move to the next level."

The Right-Minded Teamwork Model: A Legacy

Not only did Dan’s efforts deliver consistent, powerful results (gaining him many long-term clients over the years) at a higher level, but his work also positively impacted the practice of behavioral change management.

Over the course of his career, Dan refined his ideas along with the help of his clients and the teams he served. Eventually, he created his own proprietary tools, processes, and strategies. Of all his models and creations, Dan’s most significant accomplishment has been the development of his Right-Minded Teamwork model, which perfectly assembles all his tools and processes into a single, streamlined approach.

At its core, Right-Minded Teamwork (RMT) is a continuous improvement loop for small and large groups; it has been proven to work with teams of all sizes. No matter what team challenges or interpersonal issues are happening, RMT has the power to correct them.

By first bringing the team together under a unified set of goals, and then providing tools for teams to explore, understand, and work through their underlying concerns, Right-Minded Teamwork provides teams with the opportunity to address unproductive behaviors in a safe, non-condemning way. Focusing on acceptance, forgiveness, and self-adjustment among teammates, Right-Minded Teamwork directly addresses and resolves the root cause of even the most difficult teamwork situations.

After directly serving over 500 teams in seven countries and creating lasting tools and resources that will go on to support countless additional teams, leaders, and facilitators on every continent, Dan Hogan has left a legacy to be proud of. No longer an active facilitator, Dan has transformed his ideas and contributions into powerful, effective, team-building tools available online, providing team facilitators and team leaders around the globe access to Right-Minded Teamwork.

Books by Dan Hogan

Reason, Ego & the Right-Minded Teamwork Myth*: The Philosophy and Process for Creating a Right-Minded Team That Works Together as One*

This book explores two foundational concepts: the Right-Minded Teamwork Myth, a short tale that presents RMT's underlying teamwork philosophy, and the Right-Minded Teamwork team-building process, a step-by-step approach to implementing RMT in any team.

Right-Minded Teamwork in Any Team*: The Ultimate Team-Building Method to Create a Team That Works as One*

Right-Minded Teamwork is built on a framework of 5 Elements, explored in this book. These two goals and three methods are implemented into your team through three team-building workshops conducted over a six-to-12-month period. Once your team completes its third workshop, you move into a 90-day, continuous improvement operating plan that allows your team to achieve their goals, do no harm and work together as one.

How to Facilitate Team Work Agreements*: A Practical, 10-Step Process for Building a Right-Minded Team That Works as One*

Team Work Agreements are collective pledges made by your team to transform non-productive or dysfunctional actions into positive and constructive work behavior. Though this book is written primarily for team facilitators, team leaders, and teammates may also follow these steps to create powerful, effective Work Agreements to solve and prevent interpersonal and process problems.

How to Apply the Right Choice Model*: Create a Right-Minded Team That Works as One*

The concept of Right Choice states every person has free will. Free will means you are 100% responsible for how you respond to every situation, circumstance, and event. When difficult team problems occur, you either act as an ally or an adversary. When you choose to be an ally, you demonstrate positive, accountable behavior. When you are an adversary, you behave as either a victim or a victimizer. This book and model will guide you through creating a team of productive, supportive, Right-Minded teammate allies.

7 Mindfulness Training Lessons*: Improve Teammates' Ability to Work as One with Right-Minded Thinking*

If you want your team to work together as one, you want them to think as one, too. These 7 Mindfulness Training Lessons will help you achieve a positive team mindset by guiding teammates to raise their awareness of thoughts, choices, and behaviors. Teammates may also use these lessons to create the team's Right-Minded thought system. The 7 Lessons can be summed up in one sentence, emphasizing three words: Right-Minded Teammates **accept**, **forgive**, and **adjust** their thinking and work behavior. When teammates follow these lessons, they **do no harm** while **working together as one.**

Right-Minded Teamwork*: 9 Right Choices for Building a Team That Works as One*

This quick read is an excellent Right-Minded Teamwork primer and a terrific way to introduce RMT to teammates. These nine teamwork choices are universal, self-evident, and self-validating. You want them in your team. In this book, each of the 9 Right Choices is defined, and exercises are provided for applying each choice.

Design a Right-Minded, Team-Building Workshop*: 12 Steps to Create a Team That Works as One*

This book includes complete instructions on how to design a practical, real-world, team-building workshop that teammates actually want to attend. Unlike many team activities labeled "team building" that are really more "team bonding," true team-building workshops are intentionally designed to solve a team's real-world problems. Written primarily for team facilitators, team leaders, and teammates may also follow these 12 steps to design an effective, transformative team workshop.

Achieve Your Organization's Strategic Plan*: Create a Right-Minded Team Management System to Ensure All Teams Work as One*

When a single team within an organization works together as one, they are effective and productive. When an enterprise works with the same level of synergy, it is exponentially more powerful. A Team Management System like the Right-Minded Teamwork TMS model taught in this book lays the groundwork for your organization to get every team on the same page. By following RMT's four-part rollout plan, you can create and deploy your own Team Management System, align teammate attitudes, and work behavior with company values, and bring your entire organization together to work as one and achieve your strategic plan.

Glossary of Right-Minded Teamwork Terms & Resources

100% Customer Satisfaction

Creating 100% customer satisfaction is a primary goal of Right-Minded Teamwork. Your team is responsible for providing quality products and services to customers; for your team and enterprise to succeed, your customers deserve to be 100% satisfied.

With a strong customer satisfaction plan, as described in ***Right-Minded Teamwork in Any Team***, your teammates will strive to achieve customer satisfaction while consistently achieving other business goals.

7 Mindfulness Training Lessons

Achieving Right-Minded Teamwork involves adopting an attitude of mindfulness. The *7 Mindfulness Training Lessons* teach you to think in a Right-Minded way, ensuring you **do no harm** as you **work as one** with your teammates.

These powerful lessons are summed up in one sentence, with emphasis on three words:

Right-Minded Teammates ***accept, forgive,*** *and* ***adjust*** *their thinking and work behavior.*

In every circumstance, especially during difficult team situations, Right-Minded Teammates practice mindfulness to move them from defensiveness and blame into a Right-Minded, allied way of thinking and behaving.

Inspired by *A Course in Miracles* and our Right Choice Model, the *7 Mindfulness Training Lessons* is a teaching tool designed to help those willing to apply them to ensure they return to the Unified Circle of Right-Minded Thinking.

Go to RightMindedTeamwork.com or visit your favorite book retailer to pick up your copy of ***7 Mindfulness Training Lessons****: Improve Teammates' Ability to Work as One with Right-Minded Thinking.*

10 Characteristics of Right-Minded Teammates

Right-Minded Teammates have many different surface traits and personalities. They are not all alike. They have numerous backgrounds, vastly different experiences, and a wide range of skills.

Nevertheless, it is understood that the Right-Minded Teammate, in their own particular behavioral style, happily live these characteristics because they align the teammate's authentic *self* with their team's version of the RMT motto: *do no harm*, *work as one*, and *none of us is as smart as all of us*.

You will find a complete description of these characteristics in RMT's book: ***Right-Minded Teamwork in Any Team:*** *The Ultimate Team Building Method to Create a Team That Works as One.*

1. Trust	2. Honesty	3. Tolerance
4. Gentleness	5. Joy	6. Defenselessness
7. Generosity	8. Patience	9. Open-Mindedness
	10. Faithfulness	

12 Steps Workshop Design Process

Design a Right-Minded, Team-Building Workshop:*12 Steps to Create a Team That Works as One.* This book will teach you how to design a practical, real-world team-building workshop.

The 12 steps are grouped into three phases: Contract, Commence, and Carry on. Written primarily for team facilitators, team leaders, and teammates can easily follow the steps to design a successful team-building workshop. Because this method engages teammates in designing the agenda, it virtually guarantees that teammates *cannot wait* to attend the workshop. They *know* that they will get real work done in a safe, "no harm" environment when they meet.

A Course in Miracles

Oneness. Forgiveness is the key to happiness, inner peace, undifferentiated unity, and ultimately – *oneness*. "A Course In Miracles (ACIM) is a unique spiritual self-study program designed to awaken us to the truth of our *oneness* with God and Love," as posted on ACIM.org and ACIM.org/ACIM/en. See the Foundation for A Course in Miracles at FACIM.org, where Ken Wapnick, the founder, created this beautiful definition.

> *A Course in Miracles is a psychological approach to spirituality where forgiveness is the central theme, and inner peace is the result.*

ACIM and other moral and spiritual philosophies that advocate and help people everywhere ***work together as One*** has inspired Right-Minded Teamwork. We used Ken's definition as a guide to create the Right-Minded Teamwork definition.

> *Right-Minded Teamwork is a business-oriented, psychological approach to team building where acceptance, forgiveness, and adjustments are teammate characteristics, and 100% customer satisfaction is the team's result.*

All Right-Minded Teamwork methods, processes, and tools seamlessly work together to help you create and sustain a *Team That Works Together as* ***One.***

Accept, Forgive, Adjust

These three terms are at the core of Right-Minded Teammate Attitudes & Behaviors. These verbs are also central to the *7 Mindfulness Training Lessons*, which are summed up in the sentence, *Right-Minded Teammates* ***accept****,* ***forgive****, and* ***adjust*** *their thinking and work behavior.*

Furthermore, these three concepts are included in the definition of Right-Minded Teamwork:

> *Right-Minded Teamwork is a business-oriented, psychological approach to team building where* ***acceptance****,* ***forgiveness****, and* ***adjustment*** *are teammate characteristics, and 100% customer satisfaction is the team's result.*

Lastly, these terms are also incorporated as three of the five steps in the *Right Choice Model*, which describes accountable and responsible Right-Minded Teamwork behavior.

Ally or Adversary Teammate

Right-Minded Teamwork asserts that as teammates, you either work together as allies, or pull apart, viewing each other as adversaries.

Allies work towards achieving team goals. Adversaries work towards individual elevation, which separates and divides the team.

To determine whether you are in an ally or adversary mindset, ask yourself, *Do I want to be right, or do I want our team to be successful?* Allies want to be part of a successful team. Adversaries want to be right, no matter the cost.

As an adversary, Ego persuades you to compete with your teammates. As an ally, Reason says the opposite. Reason gently reminds you that separateness prevents true success. There cannot be oneness or collaboration where there is competition.

As the Decision-Maker, you choose to follow either Reason or Ego. You either collaborate or compete. You are an ally or adversary. There is no middle ground.

If you choose to follow Reason and become an ally, you embrace and live your team's Work Agreements. If you decide to follow Ego, you become an adversary, creating a battleground inside yourself and your team.

To transform competitive adversaries into collaborative allies, start by following the *Right Choice Model*, creating team *Work Agreements*, and applying the *7 Mindfulness Training Lessons*.

Avoidance Behavior

Even though the term "avoidance behavior" is not often mentioned in the Right-Minded Teamwork model or books, avoidance behavior is easy to detect in teammates and RMT processes. If you notice it occurring, from an RMT perspective, you can consider it wrong-minded, adversarial behavior.

Identifying avoidance behaviors and attitudes and understanding the harm they cause is the first step in moving from a wrong-minded place into Right-Mindedness. The *7 Mindfulness Training Lessons* and the *Right Choice Model* are excellent tools for teaching yourself and your team how to act and behave in a Right-Minded, accountable way.

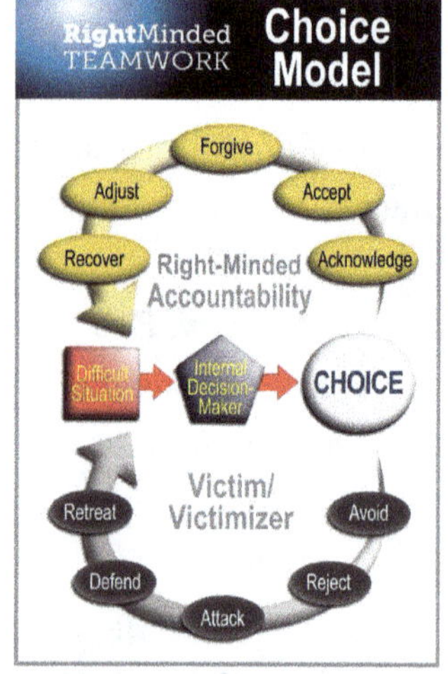

For example, if you look carefully at the *Right Choice Model's* lower loop, you will notice that the victim or victimizer first avoids the situation when a difficult situation occurs.

When Right-Minded Teammates ask themselves the *Right Choice Model* question, *How did I* ***create****,* ***promote****, or* ***allow*** *this difficult situation to happen?* they often realize they have unconsciously demonstrated avoidance behavior. Then, noticing their mistake, they simply choose to **accept**, **forgive**, and **adjust** their approach and return to living in accordance with their team *Work Agreements*.

Battleground: Where People Are Punished for Mistakes

The battleground represents wrong-minded thinking. It is a mental attitude or thought system that defends and encourages adversarial behaviors such as blame and attack.

Think of the battleground as a psychological symbol for those moments when you realize you are listening to Ego, not Reason (like when you notice avoidance behavior). You recognize that you are having an Ego attack for whatever reason and have made a wrong-minded choice. When you are in the battleground, you "punish" others for their mistakes, either by victimizing others or becoming a victim yourself.

On the other hand, when you are in your right mind, you see your team as a lovely and safe classroom, the opposite of the battleground. You do not punish others. You choose, instead, to rise above the conflict.

The purpose of recognizing the battlegrounds in your mind is to own the pain that you are causing yourself which helps you recognize that you consciously want to leave it, overlook it, rise above it, and transport your mind into the classroom where you return to the forgiving Unified Circle of Right-Minded Thinking with your teammates.

Right-Minded Teammates working in safe and supportive classrooms do not fight, blame, or punish. Instead, they choose oneness over separateness. They are committed to the team's success and achieving team goals.

To overcome a battleground in yourself or your team, go to RightMindedTeamwork.com, or visit your favorite book retailer to pick up your copy of ***How to Apply the Right Choice Model****: Create a Right-Minded Team That Works as One*. Inside, you will find a list of battleground attitudes and behaviors as well as the costs and benefits of classroom versus battleground thinking and behaving.

Certified Master Facilitator (CMF)

The Certified Master Facilitator (CMF) credential is a mark of excellence for facilitators. It is the highest available certification for facilitators. To learn more or to find a certified facilitator worldwide, visit the International Institute for Facilitation at INIFAC.org.

Classroom: Where People Learn from Mistakes

Like the battleground, the classroom is a symbol. But unlike the battlefield, where people punish or are punished, the classroom is where you learn and find inspiration.

At some point in your past, you have experienced the joy and wonder of learning. Right-Minded Teamwork invites you to view your team as a safe place to experience this wonder and joy as you learn new teamwork skills and collaborate to achieve team goals.

When you are experiencing fear in any form or realize you are having an Ego attack, you are in the battleground. To return to the classroom, say to yourself, *There is nothing to fear. In my mind, I choose to rise above this silly battleground and head to my Right-Minded classroom. There, we are committed to Do No Harm and Work as One. There, we will find solutions.*

By recognizing the fear behind your Ego attack and reminding yourself to return to the classroom, you experience a **moment of Reason**. You also strengthen your Right-Minded thought system and restore yourself to Right-Minded Thinking.

In the RMT book ***How to Apply the Right Choice Model****: Create a Right-Minded Team That Works as One,* you will find a list of 30 Right-Minded and wrong-minded attitudes and behaviors, plus the associated costs and benefits to your team.

Communication Work Agreement

What you think – *your thought system* – drives your communication in one of two ways. You either communicate as a collaborative ally or as a competitive, dysfunctional, and emotionally immature adversary.

Teams that work as one and achieve their goals regularly seek out opportunities to improve communication. They take positive action by creating and living a Communication Work Agreement that describes their team's agreed-upon communication style.

Right-Minded communication is a core concept in the book ***Right-Minded Teamwork****: 9 Right Choices for Building a Team That Works as One*, available at RightMindedTeamwork.com or your favorite book retailer.

To create your team's Communication Work Agreement, follow the suggestions in the book ***How to Facilitate Teamwork Agreements****: A Practical, 10-Step Process for Building a Right-Minded Team That Works as One*.

In there, you will find two real examples of which one is a team Communication Work Agreement.

Create, Promote, Allow

These three concepts form the foundation of the *Right Choice Model's* essential question:

*How have I **created**, **promoted**, or **allowed** this situation to occur?*

Asking and honestly answering this question ensures teammates are "owning their part" in a difficult situation.

These three concepts are also integrated into ***7 Mindful Training Lessons****: Improve Teammate's Ability to Work as One with Right-Minded Thinking.*

High-performing Right-Minded Teammates always ask themselves this question because it leads them to solutions. It is a clear demonstration of the RMT motto, "**Do no harm**. **Work as one**."

Critical Few: Complete Important Tasks First

When a team is stuck in the "full-plate syndrome," identifying and completing the critical few - those tasks that have the largest and most direct impact on the team's success - is key to moving forward.

At the root of the full-plate syndrome is the **team's collective fear**, driven by Ego, which declares you will get in trouble if you do not do it all… even though the truth is you can never do it all.

People who listen to Ego believe they do not have a choice. Rather than realistically prioritizing their workload, they punish themselves for failing to meet the unreasonable goal of completing everything. They drain their energy, lose their focus, and make mistakes. They become powerless, cynical, and burned out.

But Reason reminds us that we always have this choice:

> *We can either win by doing the critical few tasks, or we can lose by attempting to do everything.*

Spend more time doing the right things right and let go of low-value tasks. Holding on to lower-value tasks is **not security**. It is **incarceration**.

The "critical few" concept is discussed in the book ***Right-Minded Teamwork***: *9 Right Choices for Building a Team That Works as One*.

See **Recognition: Make It Easy to Keep Going** for a related concept.

Decision-Maker: The Real You

Ken Wapnick, Ph.D., created the term "Decision-Maker" to define the "real you" in *A Course in Miracles*. For more on his work, visit FACIM.org.

Within Right-Minded Teamwork, the *Right Choice Model* uses the term "Decision-Maker" to describe the part of you that chooses to listen to and follow either the wrong-minded ways of Ego or the Right-Minded ways of Reason.

Your Decision-Maker is 100% responsible for who you choose to follow, what you choose to think, and how you choose to behave.

Right-Mindedness is achieved when you listen to and follow Reason. Listening means calming your Ego mind, trusting your intuition, and allowing space for a **moment of Reason** to arise.

When Right-Mindedness becomes an integral part of a team, the team consistently works together as one, doing no harm, within the forgiving Unified Circle of Right-Minded Thinking. When teammates do that, they are demonstrating and extending Right-Minded Teamwork to everyone.

To learn more about Reason, Ego, and the Decision-Maker, visit RightMindedTeamwork.com or your favorite book retailer and pick up the book ***Reason, Ego, & the Right-Minded Teamwork Myth***: *The Philosophy & Process for Creating a Right-Minded Team That Works Together as One.*

Decision-Maker: Trust Your Intuition

If thinking about Reason and Ego are new to you, it can be helpful to think of Reason as your positive intuition and Ego as your negative, arrogant, and sometimes vindictive intuition.

At different times throughout our lives, we all have listened to and followed each of these teachers.

Stop and remember when you had a hunch or a feeling as to what you should do or say in a particular situation. Did you ignore your intuition? Let's say you did not follow your instinct, and it turned out to be a mistake. What did you say to yourself and others?

> *I wish I had trusted my intuition!*

As this memory illustrates, **you already know how to listen and be mindful** of your intuition. It is your natural, pre-separation state of mind [See **Oneness vs. Separateness**].

You just need to do it regularly.

Decision-Making Work Agreement

Every team needs a Decision-Making Work Agreement that clearly defines how decisions are made and who makes them. Creating a general agreement and putting it into your team's Operating System's Business Plan as a team Work Agreement makes good business sense.

If you do not currently have a Decision-Making team agreement or you have not updated it recently, I highly recommend you do that as soon as it is practical.

Incidentally, Decision-Making is #18 in the *Team Performance Factor Assessment* that you will use every 90 days to keep your team focused and on track. See **Team Operating System**.

In the book, ***How to Facilitate Team Work Agreements**: A Practical, 10-Step Process for Building a Right-Minded Team That Works as One,* you will find two real agreement examples. The first one is a behavioral team Communication Work Agreement, and the other is a Decision-Making Work Agreement. Check it out and use it as a model for your team's Decision-Making Work Agreement.

Desire & Willingness: Preconditions for Accountability

Even though the terms "desire" and "willingness" are not often mentioned in Right-Minded Teamwork materials (except within the *Right Choice Model*), Right-Mindedness and accountability are virtually synonymous.

The concepts of desire and willingness permeate all RMT methods and processes simply because it is impossible to think in a Right-Minded way, behave with Right-Minded Accountability, and achieve Right-Minded Teamwork without a heartfelt desire and genuine willingness to do so.

The *Right Choice Model* found in the book ***How to Apply the Right Choice Model**: Create a Right-Minded Team That Works as One* teaches, *Right-Minded Accountability is the desire and willingness to change my mind and behavior in order to effectively respond to difficult team situations.*

If you share the Right Choice Model with your team and distribute the Right Choice cards to teammates, you will see the definition of "desire and willingness" on the cards.

Do No Harm. Work as One. ®

The Right-Minded philosophy is founded on two universal truths:

None of us is as smart as all of us.
Right-Minded Teammates know that working collaboratively together, in a Right-Minded manner, is the only way to create the kind of teamwork that achieves and sustains 100% customer satisfaction.

Do No Harm and Work as One.
As a Right-Minded Teammate, you can be firm, direct, gentle, and compassionate, all at the same time. You do not blame yourself or others for mistakes. You and your teammates are allies, not adversaries, working together towards your shared goals.

Ego & Ego Attack

Ego is the negative, wrong-minded teacher who continually tells you how difficult the world is and how you must constantly fight to survive.

Reason is the opposite of Ego. Reason teaches you to *do unto others as you would have them do unto you.*

Ego believes everyone is out to get you and directs you to *do unto others before they do unto you.* Ego is also the creator of the tiny, mad idea of separation presented in the *Right-Minded Teamwork Myth.*

An Ego attack is a flash of negative, out-of-control emotion. It happens when you believe the awful feeling you are experiencing has been caused by something someone else said or did to you. Without thinking, you become behaviorally triggered; your body language, tone of voice, and the words you say become mean-spirited. An Ego attack is the opposite of a **moment of Reason**.

As soon as you realize you are experiencing an Ego attack, you must train your mind to say, *I am angry. I have lost control. I'm not upset for the reason I think. I am out of my right mind. I need a moment of Reason to gain control of my attitude. I must return to the classroom so I can find a Right-Minded way of replying that allows us to do no harm and work as one.*

Interlocking Accountability

Interlocking accountability is a crucial RMT concept that is primarily used in ***How to Facilitate Team Work Agreements****: a Practical, 10-Step Process for Building a Right-Minded Team That Works as One.*

When your team creates Work Agreements, it is highly recommended that one of your agreements includes an interlocking accountability statement so that teammates agree, ahead of time, how to compassionately confront a teammate who continues to break your Work Agreements.

Interlocking Accountability means many things, including:

- Giving positive reinforcement when someone continues to do a great job of living the Work Agreements.
- Confronting someone in a supportive and safe but firm way if they continue to break the spirit or letter of the team's Work Agreement.
- Being accountable to each other for achieving or accomplishing the desired outcome of the Work Agreements.

- Recovering and learning from mistakes rather than denying or punishing those who make mistakes. This strengthens team spirit and trust.
- Creating and sustaining teammate trust because teammates who believe everyone will live their part of the Work Agreement will create Right-Minded Teamwork.

Moment of Reason

When you are facing a challenge such as an Ego attack, and you experience a positive and perhaps surprising moment of revelation, clarity, or sanity, you have achieved a moment of Reason.

These moments occur when you genuinely try to move from the battleground into the classroom. When Reason's teaching breaks through, you move from wrong-mindedness into Right-Mindedness.

Moments of Reason are magnificent. They are a cornerstone of your Right-Minded thought system. When they happen, you feel confident and at peace. You know what you should do, what to say, and to whom.

In moments of Reason, you know beyond a shadow of a doubt that you want and need your teammates. You easily return to the Unified Circle of Right-Minded Thinking, where teammates forgive one another, do no harm, and work as one.

Onboarding New Teammates

When a new leader or teammate joins your team, it is vitally important to properly onboard them within their first week on the job. In a single short meeting where everyone attends, the onboarding is easily and effectively accomplished.

Present all your RMT goals and Work Agreements along with why they were created. They ask you clarifying questions. Afterward, you ask them to accept the team's goals and actively live the team's Work Agreements.

Oneness vs. Separateness

Oneness is a psychological state of mind. It can be described in many ways using phrases such as *None of us is as smart as all of us,* or *do no harm,* and *work as one.*

Separateness is the opposite of oneness. To become a Right-Minded teammate, you must train your mind to choose attitudes and behaviors that create and extend oneness, not project separateness.

For a list of 30 examples of oneness, see the Right-Minded Teamwork Attitudes & Behaviors list found in numerous RMT books.

The concepts and story behind oneness and separateness are introduced in RMT's book, ***Reason, Ego & the Right-Minded Teamwork Myth:*** *The Philosophy and Process for Creating a Right-Minded Team That Works Together as One.*

In this book, you will learn about Ego's "tiny, mad idea" of wanting more "stuff" and how Ego's choices led us all into a world of separation. That tiny, mad moment was, literally, the **birth of**

separation. But, as the Myth reveals, Reason is always ready to lead us back into oneness - our pre-separation state – joyfully described as the Unified Circle of Right-Minded Thinking where we can do no harm and work as one.

Preventions & Interventions

In RMT's ***Design a Right-Minded, Team-Building Workshop****: 12 Steps to Create a Team That Works as One*, the team-building facilitator and team leader meet early on to proactively identify potential issues that could keep teammates from achieving the workshop's desired outcomes.

This discussion leads to creating *preventions* that the team leader or facilitator takes to help prevent those issues from happening. The facilitator and team leader also agree on how to intervene in case the preventions don't work. Much of the time, however, preventions do their job and make *interventions* during team-building workshops unnecessary.

To learn more about effective preventions and interventions, go to RightMindedTeamwork.com or your favorite book retailer, and pick up your copy of these two books:

How to Facilitate Team Work Agreements*: A Practical, 10-Step Process for Building a Right-Minded Team That Works as One*

Design a Right-Minded, Team-Building Workshop*: 12 Steps to Create a Team That Works as One*

Psychological Goals

A team's psychological goals describe how teammates intentionally choose to think and behave as they work together to achieve their team's business goals.

Psychological goals, such as achieving mutual trust and respect among teammates, may be viewed as a team's collective school of thought, values, or thought system.

These consciously chosen goals, captured in team Work Agreements, clarify the team's principles or standards of behavior.

Here is a specific example of a psychological goal you will find in several RMT materials:

> *When difficult team situations happen, we accept, forgive, and adjust our attitudes and behavior. We always find solutions because we believe that none of us is as smart as all of us.*

Reason

Reason is a mythological character and symbolic guide who shows you how to think and behave in a Right-Minded way. As your Right-Minded teacher, Reason helps you differentiate and choose between Right-Minded and wrong-minded attitudes and behaviors.

Reason is the opposite of Ego. Whereas Ego believes everyone is out to get you and instructs you to *do unto others before they do unto you,* Reason teaches you to *do unto others as you would have them do unto you.*

Ego encourages and projects separateness.
Reason cultivates and extends oneness.

Reason is that part of your mind that always speaks for the Right Choice attitudes and behaviors. When you need a **moment of Reason** to find the best way to respond to a difficult team situation, say to yourself:

> *I am here to be truly helpful.*
>
> *I am here to represent Reason who sent me.*
>
> *I do not have to worry about what to say or what to do because Reason who sent me will direct me.*

When you experience a moment of Reason (a moment of revelation, clarity, or sanity regarding a particular challenge), "remembering" Reason's gentle guidance towards oneness restores your mind to the forgiving Unified Circle of Right-Minded Thinking.

For the full story of Ego's tiny, mad idea of separation and how Reason waits even today to bring us back to oneness, pick up your copy of the book ***Reason, Ego & the Right-Minded Teamwork Myth**: The Philosophy and Process for Creating a Right-Minded Team That Works Together as One.*

Reason, Ego & the Right-Minded Teamwork Myth

This book teaches two significant concepts:

- the Right-Minded Teamwork Myth is a short tale that presents RMT's underlying teamwork philosophy of doing no harm and working as one
- the Right-Minded Teamwork team-building tools, methods, and processes to create Right-Minded, productive teams.

The RMT Myth is a short, simple story. It follows three characters: Reason, Ego, and you, the Decision-Maker. Simply put, the RMT Myth and philosophy advocate for teammates to follow Reason's path of oneness instead of following Ego's disastrous advice to seek separateness and prioritize selfishness.

Following the RMT Myth, you will learn about the Right-Minded Teamwork process. Unlike the story, the RMT process is no myth. It is practical, deliberate, and reliable.

The RMT process is a set of interconnected, team-building methods that together form a self-perpetuating, continuous improvement system. This process allows you to integrate the aspirations of the RMT Myth into your team in a way that helps you achieve your business goals.

This book teaches the RMT process and provides a clear overview of the seven other RMT team-building books that, when used together, form a continuous improvement process guaranteed to support team growth and success.

Recognition: Make It Easy to Keep Going

Authentic recognition is not about bestowing company shirts and prizes. It is about giving and receiving genuine appreciation for a job well done.

Recognition plays a critical role in growing your team's business because it keeps your team's spirit ignited. Unfortunately, many people work in team environments where there is little to no recognition. These teammates are discouraged. They do not give their best to the team. Why should they?

Discouraged teammates are like racehorses. If a horse is giving you only 80%, you can whip him, and he will give you 90%. Whip him again, and he will give you 100%. But if you whip him again, after he has already given you everything he has, he will drop back to 80%, or maybe even less. He has learned that you are going to whip him regardless, even if he works harder. So why should he give you his best?

Whipped people leave teams.

Far too often, the ones who leave are the most talented teammates. People who receive legitimate and genuine recognition stay and contribute. Shirts and prizes cannot earn that kind of loyalty or effort.

In the book ***Right-Minded Teamwork**: 9 Right Choices for Building a Team That Works as One*, you will learn that Recognition is one of the 9 Right Choices.

See **Critical Few: Complete Important Tasks First**. for a related concept.

Right Choice Model

The *Right Choice Model* is an effective teaching aid that will help you and your teammates choose your own set of unique, "right" teamwork attitudes and behaviors.

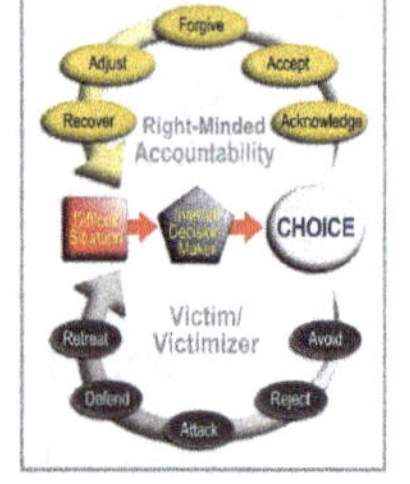

Inspired by *A Course in Miracles*, *The Right Choice Model* consists of two circles. The upper loop of acceptance, forgiveness, and adjustment represents the Unified Circle of Right-Minded Thinking.

The lower loop of rejection, Ego attack, and defensiveness describes the separated or divided circle of wrong-minded thinking.

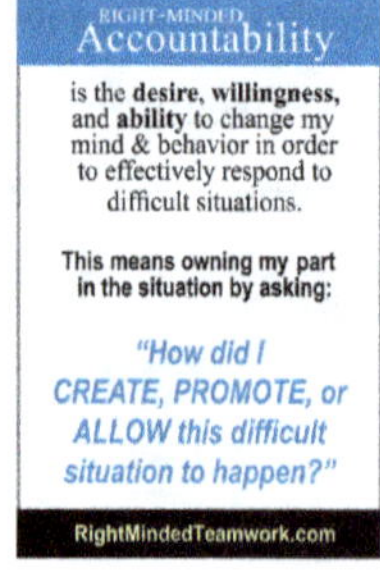

To learn more about this simple but powerful teaching model, go to RightMindedTeamwork.com or your favorite book retailer, and pick up your copy of ***How to Apply the Right Choice Model**: Create a Right-Minded Team That Works as One.*

Right-Minded Teamwork's 5-Element Framework

Right-Minded Teamwork is a business-oriented, psychological approach to team building where acceptance, forgiveness, and adjustment are teammate characteristics, and 100% customer satisfaction is the team's result.

Right-Minded Teamwork is built off a framework of 5 Elements consisting of two goals and three teamwork methods.

1. Team **Business Goal**: Achieve 100% Customer Satisfaction
2. Team **Psychological Goal**: Commit to Right-Minded Thinking
3. Team **Work Agreements**: Create & Follow Commitments
4. **Team Operating System**: Make It Effective & Efficient
5. **Right-Minded Teammates**: Strengthen Individual Performance

To learn more, go to RightMindedTeamwork.com or your favorite book retailer, and pick up your copy of ***Right-Minded Teamwork in Any Team****: The Ultimate Team-Building Method to Create a Team That Works as One*.

Right-Minded Teamwork's 5-Element Implementation Plan

There is no one right way to implement RMT's 5 Elements but the three-workshop plan presented in the book ***Right-Minded Teamwork in Any Team**: The Ultimate Team-Building Method to Create a Team That Works as One* has proven effective countless times.

Here's a brief overview.

First Workshop
Create **psychological goals** plus at least one **Work Agreement**.

Second Workshop
Reaffirm **business goals** and agree on a **team operating system**.

Third Workshop
Encourage and support Right-Minded **Teammate development**.

After the third workshop, and every 90 days after that, you will apply RMT's ***Team Operating System & Performance Factor Assessment*** to identify opportunities, take action, and achieve new teamwork improvements.

Right-Minded Teamwork
Attitudes & Behaviors

The Right-Minded Teamwork model includes a list of 30 behavioral and process-oriented teammate attitudes and behaviors with their associated costs and benefits. I collected and compiled these over three decades of team-building workshops.

This valuable list includes clear, specific, right, and wrong behaviors "taught" to us by either Reason or Ego.

Thoughts and attitudes always precede teamwork behavior. Right-Minded attitudes come from Reason. Wrong-minded attitudes come from the Ego.

The good news is that Right-Minded attitudes are natural. They are already inside you and your teammates. When you think about any of the wrong-minded Ego attitudes listed you will see in the list, ask yourself,

> *Was I born with these depressing, debilitating, and awful attitudes?*

Your answer will always be "**no!**" You learned those wrong-minded attitudes from Ego. That means ***you can unlearn them, too***.

You can find the list in several RMT books, including ***How to Apply the Right Choice Model:*** *Create a Right-Minded Team That Works as One*, available at RightMindedTeamwork.com or your favorite book retailer.

Right-Mindedness vs. Wrong-Mindedness

"Mindedness" is what you choose to think and perceive. Right-Mindedness refers to the positive mental state, perceptions, choices, and actions you demonstrate when following Reason's guidance.

Wrong-mindedness refers to the negative mental state that occurs when you follow Ego's advice.

> *Mindfulness is a journey without distance to a goal* ***you want to achieve.***

In the book ***How to Apply the Right Choice Model****: Create a Right-Minded Team That Works as One*, you will find a list of rewards and consequences for choosing Right-Mindedness.

In the book ***7 Mindfulness Training Lessons****: Improve Teammates' Ability to Work as One with Right-Minded Thinking*, you will learn that in every circumstance, and especially during difficult team situations, Right-Minded Teammates practice mindfulness, or Right-Mindedness, to move them into an ally-focused way of thinking and behaving.

Both of these books will help you accept that your mind is split between two thought systems. At one moment, you are following Reason, and the next, Ego. It is impossible to create and sustain Right-Minded Thinking with a split mind. To heal your split mind, you want to apply the *7 Mindful Training Lessons* and the *Right Choice Model's* attitudes and behaviors.

To bring your team back into the forgiving Unified Circle of Right-Minded Thinking, pick up your copy of these books at your favorite book retailer or RightMindedTeamwork.com.

RMT Facilitator

The RMT Facilitator has a special function. Simply put, their expert facilitation *transforms* well-meaning dysfunctional souls into *healthy and functional teammates*.

Using the array of RMT tools, the RMT Facilitator guides teammates in converting their team mistakes into *do-no-harm-work-as-one* attitudes and behaviors.

Teammates are perpetually grateful for the RMT facilitator's help in achieving and sustaining Right-Minded Teamwork. Some even say their RMT Facilitator *saved them.* Team leaders and teammates continually seek the RMT Facilitator's support for years to come.

Team transformations are the RMT Facilitator's **special function**.

Team Management System: An RMT Enterprise-Wide Process

An enterprise's Team Management System (TMS) aligns all teammate's attitudes and work behavior throughout the organization. An effective TMS ensures everyone is doing their part to help the organization achieve its vision, mission, and strategic goals.

RMT's Team Management System involves integrating RMT's 5-Element Framework into all teams.

1. Team **Business Goal**: Achieve 100% Customer Satisfaction
2. Team **Psychological Goal**: Commit to Right-Minded Thinking
3. Team **Work Agreements**: Create & Follow Commitments
4. **Team Operating System**: Make It Effective & Efficient
5. **Right-Minded Teammates**: Strengthen Individual Performance

To learn more, go to RightMindedTeamwork.com or your favorite book retailer, and purchase your copy of ***Achieve Your Organization's Strategic Plan**: Create a Right-Minded, Team Management System to Ensure All Teams Work as One.*

Team Operating System & Performance Factor Assessment

RMT's Team Operating System is a six-step, 90-day, continuous improvement operating system that organizes your team functions to increase the likelihood of achieving customer satisfaction.

The system also includes the *Team Performance Factor Assessment* [step 3], which you will use to help teammates identify two to three improvement opportunities every 90 days.

The 25 performance factors in this assessment are aligned with and thus measure the six steps of RMT's Team Operating System. They effectively measure all aspects of Right-Minded Teamwork.

If you want your team to operate more effectively and efficiently, apply this 90-day process after your team has completed the first three RMT workshops. For a brief explanation, see this glossary: *Right-Minded Teamwork's 5-Element Implementation Plan.*

Apply the three-workshop plan and the operating system, and you nearly guarantee your team will create Right-Minded Teamwork.

To learn the process, go to RightMindedTeamwork.com or your favorite book retailer, and pick up your copy of ***Right-Minded Teamwork in Any Team:** The Ultimate Team-Building Method to Create a Team That Works as One.*

Thought System

What you believe ***is*** your thought system. Pause and reflect on this truth, and above all, be thankful that it is true.

Whether you are consciously aware of it or not, your thought system is the lens through which you view the world. Without exception, everyone has one. And though there are many variations, there are ***only two thought systems*** from which to choose:

- A Right-Minded thought system, which extends ally beliefs of acceptance, forgiveness, and adjustment to everyone, everywhere, forever
- A wrong-minded system, which projects adversarial assaults of rejection, attack, and defensiveness to everyone, everywhere, forever

Once you have developed a thought system of any kind, you live it and teach it. Even if you are not entirely aware of it, it remains at the forefront of your mind, influencing your daily behaviors and choices.

If your thought system is negative, or you choose to follow Ego into an unnecessary and adversarial competition, you cannot be a happy, successful teammate.

To live in the land of oneness where your workplace is a safe and supportive classroom and where you and your teammates work as one to achieve team goals, you must train your mind and align your thought system with the teachings of Reason.

There is no possible compromise between these two thought systems. You either collaborate, or you compete. When you follow Ego, you take your team to the battleground. When you choose to follow Reason, you willingly create and genuinely strive to live your team's Work Agreements. With Reason's help, you transform your team into a lovely, collaborative, successful classroom.

The choice is clear.

Reject Ego. Embrace Reason.

Be Thankful.

Train Your Mind

When your mind is well-trained in Reason's Decision-Making ways, Ego attacks do not throw you off course. When a difficult team situation happens, you immediately stop for a **moment of Reason**. You refocus on oneness, rise above the battleground, and remember to live your Work Agreements in your classroom.

To train your mind simply means practicing your team's Work Agreements, which represent your psychological goals, as often as possible, especially during difficult team situations.

Uncovering Root Cause

The Right-Minded Teamwork philosophy advocates leaders, teammates, and facilitators resolve the root cause of teamwork issues instead of making the mistake of addressing symptoms.

Though this view is discussed in many RMT materials, uncovering the root cause is heavily emphasized as a core concept in the book ***Design a Right-Minded, Team-Building Workshop****: 12 Steps to Create a Team That Works as One*.

Inside that book, you will find a story about a well-meaning team leader who asked me, as their team-building facilitator, if I could teach a three-day workshop in just two days. He believed a quick team event would address the problem he saw in his team.

But the problem he was seeing was only the symptom, not the root cause of the issue. Had I agreed and given him what he asked for, the team would still be struggling with the same issue. And, as a facilitator, I would have failed both the team and the leader.

Instead, by pausing to look for the root cause of the team challenge first, we ended up designing and executing a practical, Right-Minded Teamwork workshop to solve the actual underlying problem.

By seeking out the root cause first, we delivered the leader's desired result, even though the workshop we held was not what he had initially asked for.

To improve your ability to uncover root causes and read this short story, go to your favorite book retailer or RightMindedTeamwork.com and pick up your copy of ***Design a Right-Minded, Team-Building Workshop****: 12 Steps to Create a Team That Works as One*.

Unified Circle of Right-Minded Thinking

When your team discusses and agrees on your psychological goals – your consciously chosen set of attitudes and behaviors as described in your Work Agreements – you have created your team's collective thought system.

By uniting with each other in this way and openly committing to one another through your Work Agreements, you are renouncing Ego in yourself and your teammates and collectively committing to train your minds to follow Reason.

This process of creating team Work Agreements is your undivided declaration of interdependence. Your assertion is saying,

> *We hold these mindful truths to be self-evident that all minds are created equal, and whosoever believes that will have everlasting freedom to choose Right-Minded Teamwork.*

Your declaration plus your daily acts of living your team Work Agreements ***is your return*** to the forgiving Unified Circle of Right-Minded Thinking.

Work Agreements

A Work Agreement is a collective promise made by teammates to transform non-productive, adversarial behavior into collaborative teamwork behavior. Work Agreements are a key tool for teammates and teams who aspire to do no harm and work as one.

Work Agreements are not flimsy ground rules. They are emotionally mature work performance commitments. Work Agreements announce your dedication to oneness and demonstrate your inner belief that *none of us is as smart as all of us.*

Your team's collective Work Agreements also define your team's psychological goals and thought system. They ensure you conduct your day-to-day work from within your team's Unified Circle of Right-Minded Thinking.

To learn more about the power of Work Agreements and how to use them to transform your team, go to RightMindedTeamwork.com or your favorite book retailer, and pick up your copy of ***How to Facilitate Team Work Agreements****: A Practical, 10-Step Process for Building a Right-Minded Team That Works as One*.

Resources

To download RMT models and processes to give teammates, go to RightMindedTeamwork.com, and search for this book's companion ***Reusable Resources & Templates***.

Reusable Resources
& Templates

for

Right-Minded Teamwork In Any Team

FIVE ELEMENTS

The Ultimate Team Building Method to Create a Team That Works as One

DAN HOGAN

Right-Minded Teammate Development - 3 Exercises

1. Trust Dialogue

The goal of this exercise is to increase and sustain teammates' trust in one another.

---

2. About Me & My Preferences

The goal of this exercise is to increase teammates' understanding of each other's work preferences. It is much faster than conducting a personality-type-style workshop, and in most cases, it is more effective.

---

3. Defining Roles and Responsibilities Using 4 Questions

The goal of this exercise is to clarify and define teammate roles and responsibilities using four questions. Doing this will increase your team's likelihood of achieving 100% customer satisfaction.

Trust Dialogue Team-Building Exercise

Go to RightMindedTeamwork.com to download, and search by its title.

The Goal

This real-world Trust Dialogue Team-Building Exercise aims to increase and sustain teammates' trust in one another.

This is an effective and impactful exercise. If you are not already an experienced team-building facilitator, it is recommended you ask a qualified facilitator to lead this exercise. There is a slight possibility it could upset some teammate relationships rather than improve them.

That said when the workshop is correctly set up and teammates are emotionally and psychologically ready, this exercise, conducted in an all-hands meeting, ***will become one of the best team-building practices*** you have ever witnessed.

Below is all you need to know for setting up and facilitating this workshop.

Trust Dialogue Outline & Process

At least one week before the workshop, the team leader and facilitator conduct a **Teammate Announcement and Preparation Meeting**.

- There, you will discuss the benefits of increasing and sustaining teammate trust within your team.

- You will also discuss and agree on the desired outcome for the workshop and team-building exercise. (See a sample Agenda below.)

- Everyone at the meeting agrees that all teammates will attend and complete their individual **Teammate Trust Dialogue Preparation Worksheet** before the workshop.

- Teammates understand that their dialogues will be conducted in pairs. Teammates agree to communicate their thoughts and feelings compassionately. Additionally, the dialogues will likely result in the creation of individual or team Work Agreements.
    - Ideally, every teammate will conduct a trust-building dialogue with every other teammate, but there may not be enough time in a single workshop.

- The team leader will decide before the workshop if the teammates are to complete the worksheet on all teammates or narrow it down to specific teammate pairs. If the latter option is chosen, teammates will agree to meet another time to ensure all teammates conduct the trust dialogue.

Teammate Announcement & Preparation Meeting

The team leader and facilitator will co-lead this meeting at least one week before the workshop. They will present and discuss most, if not all, of the following.

- Discuss the benefits of increasing and sustaining teammate trust in your team and why the leader decided to use this exercise and facilitator.

- Present, clarify, and agree that all teammates are committed to improving teammate trust.

- Go over how teammates will communicate their thoughts and feelings in their teammate dialogues.

- Remind teammates how to effectively describe trusting behaviors and encourage them to use those behaviors as building blocks for individual or team Work Agreements.

- Next, teammates are instructed on how to complete the **Teammate Trust Dialogue Preparation Worksheet**. See below.

- Eventually, each teammate will create a worksheet for every teammate.

- In this preparation meeting, the team leader will facilitate a short discussion as to what the words **candid**, **listening**, and **partnering** mean. These words and concepts are in the worksheet and the trust dialogue itself.

- Teammates will break out into pairs, sitting face to face. During the workshop's private dialogues, you will share your worksheet information with your teammate.

- One person will share their Trust Dialogue Worksheet information. Clarifying questions will be asked. Understandings are reached. Both teammates will create any needed Work Agreement(s). This first dialogue will take 15 - 20 minutes.

- Next, the second teammate shares their Trust Dialogue Worksheet and repeats the process. Once again, both teammates discuss and create Agreements.

- One round is completed when both teammates have finished their dialogue. It can take as little as 30 minutes to complete one round. Don't rush. But you don't need to talk for an hour.

- After each round, teammates switch partners and then begin the next round.

Team Leader and Facilitator Statements

Here are several statements the leader and facilitator might say during the preparation meeting.

> *All of us want and need to trust one another because we work better together when we trust each other. This exercise will help us increase and sustain our mutual trust.*
>
> *We will be conducting one-on-one dialogues in an all-hands team workshop on [date]. In those dialogues, you will discuss and agree on how you and your teammates will increase or sustain trust in one another.*
>
> *The discussion will result in a greater understanding of one another and may result in an individual Work Agreement between two team members or even a team Work Agreement.*

About Trust & Behavior

> *Trust comes from our judgment.*
>
> *We judge ourselves by our intentions, but we judge others by their behaviors. In this exercise, we will share our intentions and describe behaviors in one-on-one dialogues.*
>
> *REMEMBER: Be sure you effectively describe work behaviors and not attitudes. A behavior is something you SEE someone do or HEAR what someone says. It is also what they do NOT DO or do NOT SAY.*

An attitude is a judgment. It is not a behavior. However, you may choose to describe a behavior and then say it leads you to a specific attitude or judgment.

Here is a positive example and a negative example. When I arrive at work, you always say hello and ask me how I am doing. You are a really nice person. The "hello" is the behavior, and the "nice person" is the attitude or judgment.

Yesterday, when we were discussing XXX, you raised your voice, and pointed your finger at me, and said, 'Stop talking! You really need to control your anger. The behaviors are "raising your voice" and saying "stop talking." The "control your anger" statement is a judgmental attitude.

In fact, that last statement is an attack, one of the victim steps in the Right Choice Model. We will not make a statement like this in our trust dialogue workshop. Instead, you can say something like this: Yesterday, when we were discussing XXX, you raised your voice, and you pointed your finger at me and said, Stop talking. Maybe I was talking too much, and I think you would agree that raising our voices and pointing fingers will not resolve our conflict or improve trust. Can we find a new way to discuss issues like this in the future?

About Teammate Preparation

We must come prepared for this exercise. Here is the Trust Dialogue Worksheet. [See Below]. Before the workshop, complete the worksheet on all teammates (or a select sub-group of specific teammates). On the worksheet, you will see three criteria for trust: ***candidness*****,** ***listening,*** *and* ***partnering****.*

Being candid *means, we are straightforward, forthcoming, and impartial, without pretense or prejudice. It also means we are willing to say we were wrong, which demonstrates our willingness to admit errors in judgment or interpretation.*

Listening *means tuning in with our whole body and being intentionally emphatic. Listening well is often indicated by rephrasing and reflecting the speaker's ideas, comments, or feelings back to them. One of the most precious gifts we can give one another is the gift of being heard.*

Partnering *happens when team members feel genuinely supported and encouraged by their teammates. Partnering allows team members to make mistakes and learn from them.*

If we become less candid, don't listen, or distance ourselves from a teammate (not partnering), we lose trust in one another. This Trust Dialogue Exercise will help us avoid these damaging behaviors as we create more collaborative trust within our team.

If we do this exercise well, do you (the team) believe we will improve our trust? And are you willing to do your part as best you can? Typically, team members all say yes to both questions. Their verbal buy-in helps create accountability.

Teammate Trust Dialogue Preparation Worksheet

Instructions: Create one worksheet for every teammate.

Date: ___________
My Teammate Partner: ______________________
My Name: ______________________

I feel you are ____% **candid** in your communications with me.

I feel ____% **listened** to by you when we speak.

I feel ____% **partnered** with you when we interact.

My Request of my teammate partner

I would be better able or more willing to increase my trust with you if you would (do more, do less, stop/start) this behavior(s): _________

I will also (do more, do less, stop/start) this behavior(s) so as to increase our trust of one another: ___________

Our Work Agreement

My teammate partner and I agree to (do more, do less, stop/start) this behavior(s): ______________________.

My teammate partner and I agree that we will increase our trust in one another if we do this well.

Facilitating Trust Dialogue Workshop

Team Leader and Facilitator Statements

Imagine you are five minutes into your workshop. The team leader has welcomed everyone. All teammates have agreed to the desired outcomes, agenda, ground rules, and logistics.

Consider taking a few more moments, perhaps five minutes, to introduce the **Right Choice Model**. Your goal is to present the Model in such a way that when you finish teaching it, all teammates declare,

> *Of course, we want to approach this trust dialogue exercise in a Right-Minded, accountable way. Let's get started.*

To learn about the Right Choice Model, go to RightMindedTeamwork.com or your favorite book retailer, and pick up ***How to Apply the Right Choice Model***: *Create a Right-Minded Team That Works as One*. Look for the section titled: How to Present & Apply the Right Choice Model in Your Team. In that book, you will be given specific instructions on how to present the model successfully.

Here are several additional comments the leader and facilitator could share at the beginning of the workshop.

> *The dialogues you have today will help our team increase and sustain trust.*
>
> *Your dialogues will increase your understanding of one another and will result in new Work Agreements.*
>
> *When you say to your teammate that you could increase your trust in them if they did this or that, be sure to describe behaviors and not attitudes and ask if they would be willing to honor your request. If they say yes, you must allow them to ask you clarifying questions.*
>
> *No matter what, do not get defensive. Use reflective listening such as saying, 'So what I hear you saying is ____. Did I get it right?*

Advocate, Inquire/Ask, Disagree

Here are some additional phrases you may use to help create a positive trust dialogue between yourselves.

To **Advocate** for something, say:

> *Here's what I'm thinking and how I got there...*
> *Some of the assumptions I've made are...*
> *I reached the conclusion I did because...*
> *Here's who will be affected by my request, how they will be affected, and why...*

To **Inquire** or **Ask**, say

> *What data are you using to reach that conclusion?*
> *What's leading you to make that conclusion?*
> *What would this mean to...?*
> *Can you give me an example?*

When you **Disagree**, say

> *Tell me again how you came to believe this point of view.*
> *Are you using any data I may not have considered?*
> *Am I understanding correctly, what you're saying...?*
> *I'm having difficulty with "X", because of this reasoning...*

Trust Dialogue Meeting Agenda

Desired Outcome: Building Teammate Trust

Agenda

- Kick-off: Agree on the Desired Outcome
- Dialogue Instructions & Group Discussion
- Breakout in pairs for Round #1
- Breakout for Round #2
- Round #3
- Reconvene & Debrief as a full team
- Close

About Me & My Preferences Team-Building Exercise

Go to RightMindedTeamwork.com to download, and search by its title.

The Goal

The goal of this real-world **About Me & My Preferences Team-Building Exercise** is to increase teammates' understanding of each other's work preferences.

I used this exercise many times in my team-building practice. It was a wildly successful exercise. It never failed. And it is much faster than conducting a personality-type-style workshop.

In most cases, it was actually more effective than personality workshops because teammates addressed their most important work preferences. Doing that means they can create meaningful **Work Agreements** to build and sustain Right-Minded Teamwork.

Do this exercise, and you will be following Reason's Right-Minded Teamwork philosophy of **Do No Harm** and **Work as One**.

Exercise Instructions

- Teammates choose one, maybe two, of the questions below to answer.
- They bring their answers to a **team meeting that all teammates** attend.
- Each teammate shares at least one answer.
- Other teammates ask clarifying questions.
- If appropriate, the team or individual teammates will create Work Agreements to resolve identified challenges.
- IMPORTANT: Conduct this conversation in a collaborative and compassionate spirit. Find ways to work with another's preferences. Do not try to change another teammate.
- Remember: Right-Minded Teammates do no harm and work as one.

Preferences Exercise Questions

1. How would you describe your work style? What works or does not work well when it comes to interacting with you and your work style?
2. If another teammate thinks you are about to make a mistake, what is the best way for them to respond or call it to your attention? And what will be your responsibility?
3. What is the best way for others to express disagreement or alternative opinions without offending you? And what will be your responsibility if they don't?
4. What are your pet peeves? What makes you mad? If you are triggered, what is the best way for you and the other person to recover?
5. The biggest mistake another teammate can make with me is _________, and the best way we can recover is __________.
6. The best way to communicate with me is __________, and the best way to motivate me is __________.

Defining Teammate Roles and Responsibilities Exercise Using 4 Questions

Go to RightMindedTeamwork.com to download, and search by its title.

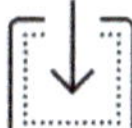

The Goal

Defining teammate roles and responsibilities using these four questions will increase your team's likelihood of achieving 100% customer satisfaction.

Many teams go off the rails because they don't know how to define and clarify teammate roles and responsibilities, or they simply don't take the time to make them clear.

Certainly, it doesn't have to be that way.

Sustainability

Clarifying teammate roles is a sure way to sustain high-performance teamwork, and this four-question roles and responsibilities workshop is faster and better than creating a RACI Matrix.

Similarly, as preventive maintenance ensures your car runs properly, conducting a periodic team-building workshop to re-clarify teammate roles and responsibilities will do the same for your team.

Why Clarify Teammate Roles?

If you don't perform "maintenance," teammates will start acting like an old, clunky car. Without clarity, they burn oil and blow smoke.

Periodic role calibration ensures your team is focused on doing the right things right. Conducting this exercise in a team meeting or team-building workshop will allow you to:

- Ensure everyone understands and accepts their role, responsibility, and accountability.
- Give positive appreciation to team members for providing resources and support so other teammates may meet or exceed their responsibilities.
- Modify and agree on new and better ways to execute individual roles within the team.

Teammate Preparation

To prepare for this exercise, teammates will answer four questions:

1. Name the **top three key** deliverables, objectives, or products you produce for the team.

2. What resources or support do you need that **you are currently receiving?**

3. What resources or support do you need that you **are not currently receiving?**

4. What are **you getting that you don't need**? What is hurting your performance?

Teammates should be prepared to offer positive changes and suggestions to improve their roles as well as the roles of others.

They should also be ready to provide solutions as to how they can get what they need or how they can let go of what they don't need.

Leader's Guide

Before the meeting, the team leader:

1. Sets a date for the exercise and invites all team members.

2. Let all team members know participation is required.

3. Distribute questions to teammates one to two weeks before the workshop date.

4. Ask teammates to write their answers to all four questions.

5. Print copies of those answers and distribute them to teammates in the workshop.

6. Ask teammates to review their answers before the workshop and to come prepared to discuss and agree with fellow teammates.

7. Ask teammates to watch this six-minute video. Dan will explain the Roles Exercise and discuss the importance of the attitude of teammate Oneness. Go to RightMindedTeamwork.com. Search for *"Define Teammate Roles Responsibilities with just four questions."*

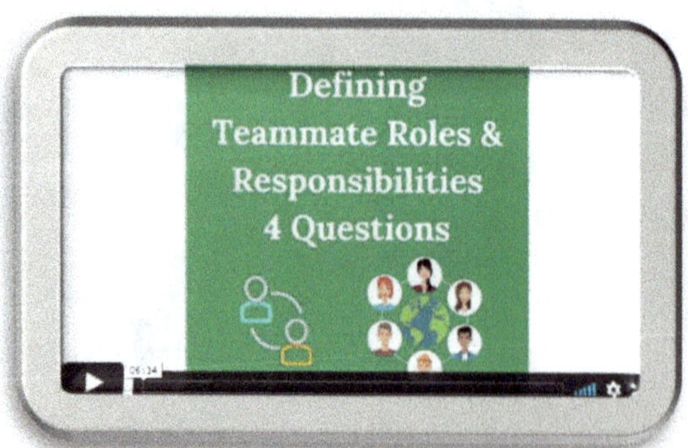

During the meeting, the team leader or facilitator:

1. Presents workshop outcomes and invites teammates to agree.

2. Ensures all teammates understand the goal of exercise. (An excellent way to do this is to ask a teammate to explain it, then allow others to comment.)

3. Obtains agreement that clear roles and responsibilities will help ensure they work and behave as one unified team.

4. Presents group exercise instructions:
    - One teammate will give their answers to all four questions, without interruption, in one to two minutes.
    - Open dialogue will follow to validate and constructively challenge their views.
    - That teammate will enjoy receiving appreciation from fellow teammates.
    - All will agree on how their teammate will get what they need or let go of what they don't need.
    - The team will document all key agreements and understandings.
    - When the first teammate's discussion is complete, the second teammate will give their answers.

5. Keeps teammates engaged (so no one is absent or brushes off the activity).

6. Help the team agree on how they will track progress and when they will recalibrate team roles again.

7. Schedules a second meeting to complete the exercise if time runs short.

After the meeting:

1. At the next few team meetings, the team leader asks all teammates, "Are we honoring and following our agreed-upon roles and responsibilities?"

Role Clarification Meeting Agenda

Desired Outcome: Discuss, clarify, confirm, and agree on who does what, when, and how.

Time Commitment: 2-4 hours

Participants:7 teammates

Agenda

A. Kick-off
B. Agree on the Desired Outcome
C. Agree to believe and behave as one unified team
D. RMT's Role Clarification exercise
    - One person at a time gives answers to the questions.
    - Dialogue follows.
    - Time permitting, create new Work Agreements & teammate understandings
    - Capture conclusions in the Team Business Plan.
    - If you run out of time, complete as many as possible, then schedule a second session to continue.
E. Close

Benefits of Ongoing Feedback

Goals + Feedback = Success

Goals give people direction, and clear roles and responsibilities are a form of goals. But goals alone aren't enough. The following study shows how feedback can make a tough goal feel more achievable. It illustrates the practical logic of providing ongoing, clear feedback.

A group of soldiers endured weeks of arduous training to qualify for elite combat units. At the end of the training, a final challenge remained: a forced march in full gear.

The soldiers were divided into four groups. Each group would march 20 kilometers (about 13 miles) over exactly the same terrain on the same day. The only variation was that each group received different instructions.

The first group was told, "You'll march 20 kilometers" (the actual distance). These soldiers received regular progress reports along the route.

The second group was given less information: "This is the long march you heard about." Group members didn't know how far they would march, nor were they informed of their progress along the way.

The third group was given an underestimation: "You'll march 15 kilometers." But after marching 14 kilometers, they were told they had six more to go.

The fourth and final group received an overestimation: "You'll march 25 kilometers." After marching 14, they were told they had only six more to go.

The results were clear. Researchers found that the first group performed the best. Knowing how far they were going and receiving regular progress reports helped the soldiers complete the 20-kilometer course the fastest, with the least stress.

Group two had the slowest time and endured more stress than all the other groups. With no idea how far they were going - only that it was a "long march" - and no feedback on their progress, group two's morale and performance suffered.

Interestingly, though groups three and four received incorrect feedback, they still outperformed group two.

Apparently, any feedback improves morale.

***Source**: Encouraging The Heart, James M. Kouzes, and Barry Z. Posner, Jossey Bass Publishers, 350 Sansome St. San Francisco, CA 94104*

Whether entirely accurate or not, feedback tells team members they're making progress toward goals and are living up to expectations. It reminds them someone cares enough about them to keep them informed.

More About Roles: The RACI Matrix

For a more detailed and complex role exercise, try the Responsibility Assignment Matrix. It is a powerful tool for clarifying the way team members work together.

I facilitated many RACIs in my career. The following RACI chart was used to define the responsibilities of all employees involved in a plant operations maintenance process.

Sometimes, this model is called RACI, which stands for:
R = Responsible
A = Accountable
C = Consulted
I = Informed

	Maintenance Management Process	Create Work Orders	Plan WOs	Approval	Procure Material	Receive Material	Schedule WOs	Assign Work	Prepare Equipment & Permits	Complete Work	Safety Activities	Maintenance Reports	Cost Control/Budget Preparations	RCFAs	RCM Analysis	MOCs	PMs	PM Job Plans	PdM Data Collection	PdM Data Analysis	CBM Action Item WOs
RC Manager	A	R	C	A	C		R	I	I		R/A	R/A	R/A	A	A	R	A	I	A	C/I	A
Maintenance Engineer	R	R	R	R	R	I	R	I	I	R/A	R	R	R	R	R	R	R	R		R	R
Reliability Engineer	R	R	C		C		I	I		C	R	I	C	R	R	R	R	R/A	R	R/A	R
Maintenance Planner	R		R/A	I	R/A	R	C				R	I	R			R	R	C			R
Maintenance Scheduler	R	R	I	I	I	A	R/A	R	I		R	R	R			C/I	R	C	R		C
Maintenance Coordinator	R	R	R	I	R	R	C	R/A	R	R	R	I	R	C		C/I	R	C	R		R
Maintenance Specialist	R	R	R		R	R	I	I	I	R	R	C	R	C	C	C	C	C		C	
Production Tech	R	R					C/I		R	C/I		I		C/I	C/I						
Plant Manager	R	R/A	C/I	R	C/I		R	I	A	C/I	R	I	R	C/I	R	A	R	I	R	I	R

RMT Implementation Plan – 4 Actual Examples

Example #1 Nuclear Power Generating Plant

Results: The senior leadership team created and deployed a 100-day Behavioral Outage that transformed the employee culture. Using RMT's Work Agreement process and other tools, this courageous **improvement project** succeeded and was featured in *Nuclear News*.

Example #2 Field Support Team

Results: This self-managing team, in one year, increased its teammate trust by 78% and saved their organization $350,000 when they successfully used RMT's **behavioral Work Agreement** process and the Three Workshop Implementation Plan.

Example #3 International Project Team

Results: This major capital project team immediately saved $10,000 a week in labor costs when they successfully used RMT's **process Work Agreement** to streamline their meetings.

Example #4 Architectural Design Company

Results: This firm had a good problem. Their business revenue had increased 100% in the past twelve months. They grew from 50 to 100 employees practically overnight, and they were still growing. They needed a strategic plan and operating structure. Using **RMT's Three Workshop Implementation Plan** plus team **Work Agreements**, they succeeded.

Example #1

The first example describes our work with a nuclear power generating plant with 500 employees. They used many RMT processes – specifically team Work Agreements and the Right Choice "Accountability" Model.

This example is presented here a little differently than the other three. After you read a short synopsis, you will read an industry article from *Nuclear News* that describes the seven behavioral modifications that compromised what they named their **100-Day Behavior Outage**.

Examples #2 - #4

I will show you how these teams used the Right-Minded Teamwork Three-Workshop Implementation Plan to achieve team improvement in the last three examples. Specifically, you will see what they accomplished in their **First** Workshop plus their **Second** and **Third** Workshops.

For each team, you will find a short description of what the team did as well as their actual Team Business Plan.

You don't need to conduct a detailed review of each plan.

Instead, use these plans as templates. These examples will give you positive ideas about creating your own Right-Minded Teamwork Implementation Plan and your Team Business Plan.

Example #1: Nuclear Power Generating Plant
Prairie Island's 100-day Behavior Outage

Synopsis

Facing a potential shutdown from their credentialing agency after a significant performance decline, Joel Sorensen, Vice President of the Prairie Island Nuclear Power Plant, knew things needed to change. So, he implemented Right-Minded Teamwork's Work Agreements and Right Choice "Accountability Model to support the plant-wide culture change plan.

Be sure to read Joel's comments in the second modification about accountability and work agreements.

"If you had asked me 2 months ago if the leadership team would reach this level of performance, my answer would have been emphatically, "NO!" Now that we are on this road, I don't ever want to go back." ~ Joel Sorensen

Joel gave this interview to the *Nuclear News* that tells the story.

THE NUCLEAR NEWS INTERVIEW

Prairie Island's 100-day Behavior Outage

Changing employees' culture requires a site-wide plan and site-wide participation.

A 100-day outage at Prairie Island didn't shut down power production, but it did change the way the plant operates. Called a "Behavior Outage," the program was aimed at altering employee culture at Prairie Island. The outage ran from last August to November and was modeled after refueling and maintenance outages in having specific plans and goals.

The Behavior Outage has helped reduce human performance errors at Prairie Island. Outage plans called on employees to examine their attitudes while changing behaviors that contributed to unpredictable performance. ***Joel Sorensen***, Prairie Island's site vice president, and his management team developed the concept for the Behavior Outage. They initiated it by first calling for an assessment of plant operations to highlight those areas where improvements were most needed. These included change management communications, accountability, leadership, human performance work practices, corrective action, work management, and outage preparation.

The two-unit Prairie Island plant, in Red Wing, Minn., is operated by Nuclear Management Company (NMC). The two units are Westinghouse pressurized water reactors, each rated at 535-MWe (net). The interview was conducted by Rick Michal, NN's senior associate editor.

Could you explain the history of the Behavior Outage at Prairie Island?

I solicited some retired nuclear executives to help me understand where our organization was going, and whether it was improving or not. Those executives came to Prairie Island the first week of August 2000 and did a self-assessment. As a result, a report they prepared showed that while plant performance had improved over the short term, our organizational effectiveness had been flat for a long time and was remaining flat. We used that report to spur our organization to break out of past behaviors and start moving ahead. The assessment showed that in order for us to have good long-term plant performance, we needed to have good behaviors on the part of our workers, managers, and supervisors.

How did you come up with 100 days for the outage?

We felt we needed to put some urgency on this. We didn't want another plan that would take months and months to execute and where we wouldn't see results. So, we decided to put together a plan to work on behaviors and get results within 100 days. Once we decided on a plan that had a sense of urgency, we decided to treat it like we would a plant refueling outage. For the Behavior Outage, there would be specific outage plans, outage schedules, and daily outage meetings to follow our progress. We patterned it after a refueling outage because we needed a similar way of doing business to get the results we wanted for our behaviors. We felt we could keep both units running safely while spending 100 days focusing on our behaviors.

What did it cost Prairie Island to conduct this outage, and did you bring in an outside vendor to help conduct it?

It doesn't cost much money to work on behaviors. We formed employee cross-disciplinary teams to help develop plans for each of the seven focus areas we identified that needed improvement. These seven areas we called "behavior modifications." But we needed help because we were struggling with accountability as a behavior. So, we partnered with a private firm—**Lord & Hogan LLC, based in Houston, Texas [creator of Right-Minded Teamwork]**—to help us understand what accountability means and to work with us on accountable behaviors.

Could you talk specifically about your seven behavior modifications?

Most emphasis on behavior modification was put on our management team as leaders of the plant, but every part of the organization, from supervisors to workers, was engaged in this activity. I'll explain each modification individually:

Our first modification is change management communications because we lacked a consistent way of implementing change. We put in place a change management model, which contains a step-by-step process, and we use it to implement all other changes we need to make. We also realized that communication had to be effective in order to instill these behavior changes across the organization, so we focused on improving internal communications between plant departments. The plan includes a mix of print, electronic, and face-to-face methods—with a strong emphasis on increased frequency of communications and greater supervisor communication with employees.

The second modification is accountability. During the 100 days, we worked on developing accountability agreements [now called **team Work Agreements**], which laid out how our managers should treat each other with regard to trust and respect. We also empowered a cross-section of employees to go out and train their peers on the meaning of accountability. There is no financial incentive for living up to the accountability agreement, but what we find is that when we live by these agreements, work becomes much more rewarding. We continue to adopt accountability agreements throughout the rest of the organization.

The **third modification** is leadership, and assessments were done for our entire leadership team. Every station manager received an assessment of his or her strengths and weaknesses. Each manager then developed a personal development plan, and they are now living and working on that plan.

The **fourth modification** is human performance work practices. We put together two teams, one being a cross-section of workers and the other a cross-section of supervisors, that developed a common set of tools for use by plant employees to prevent human error events. These tools are self-checking, procedure use and adherence, communication standards, peer-checking, and "tail-gating" sessions.

Each **week during** the Behavior Outage we focused on one of these tools to help us understand how to use it in preventing human errors. For example, the "tail-gating" session is something we want all of our employees to work through before they start any task. We want them to be able to summarize the task, anticipate what might go wrong, foresee any consequences, and evaluate what tools could be used to prevent errors. It's a mental checklist for them to use and to discuss with their co-workers before they go out on any task.

Peer checking, of all of the tools, is the one I'm most impressed with regarding how the team came up with it. Peer-checking is common in the industry, but the twist our folks put on it is by actively caring. Generally, people in Minnesota are viewed as near the top in the nation in caring. To carry this active caring to the nuclear plant was innovative and something we continue to build on.

Our behaviors prior to the 100-day outage were "conflict avoidant," which meant that people would avoid conflict. But that has changed. I'll give you an example. A general laborer here recently confronted an operator who was standing above the top safety step on a ladder. This entry-level laborer said to the veteran operator, "Hey, you're not following the ladder safety practices. Why don't you let me help you down and I will help you find a ladder that is the right height for this job." Prior to this, it would have been easy for the laborer to walk by and not confront the operator on the ladder. But when that operator got down from the ladder, he turned to the laborer and said, "Thank you."

The **fifth modification** is corrective action, which plays off putting our accountability behaviors into practice. As an entire organization, we were allowing our corrective action backlog to become overdue, knowing it would grow. But strictly by using highly accountable behavior, we were able to complete 1410 corrective actions and 917 procedure changes in our backlog. We reduced our overdue items from about 300 corrective actions that were overdue to zero. These were all completed during the 100-day Behavior Outage. This was done strictly by holding people accountable, and by completing things when we said we would complete them.

The **sixth modification** is work management. Our human performance staff told us that if we didn't fix our work management process, we'd never be able to eliminate human performance events or equipment performance events. Our existing process had been burdensome and ineffective, so we put together a team to overhaul work management. That team learned we didn't have to start from scratch. There were already some good standard processes laid out here and we just needed to work on implementing them. The team put together an implementation plan within the 100 days by using our change management plan process. We are working now to implement the team's plan completely.

The **seventh modification** is outage preparation. In the past, we would allow outage milestones to come and go and not be met. But through accountability, we were, for example, able to make sure we met our pre-outage milestones in preparing for Unit 1's refueling outage last January. For that outage, we achieved approximately a 21 percent reduction in overall outage length compared to our refueling over the previous 10 years encompassing 11 refueling outages. Much of that reduction was due to the preoutage preparation. I also credit it to the accountability behaviors on the part of our staff that executed the refueling outage—getting people to own issues, take actions, and commit to completion dates. I saw good results during the outage in the area of emergent issues that came up. Because of these accountable behaviors, we were able to identify, own, and correct emergent issues so they didn't become threats to the outage schedule.

How did the employees react when they were told there was going to be a Behavior Outage?

We had to create dissatisfaction with the status quo. I wanted everyone dissatisfied with the current state of affairs, the state of our organizational ineffectiveness. What we did was gather all the employees together for a "fire and brimstone" meeting to let them know we were not satisfied with the way things were working at Prairie Island. We all needed to change, including me.

We then laid out the plan and a new vision for the facility that focused on the long term. We had to get people thinking about what we needed to do to be an industry leader. We then set the plan in place, worked the plan, and at the end of the outage we celebrated the accomplishments.

As you went deeper into the Behavior Outage, did you see the culture changing among employees?

We, as an organization, started reading everything we could on changing culture. We recognized that our organization followed what the textbooks said about change: Roughly 20 percent of the organization jumps on board immediately and is helpful as change agents, about 50 percent of the organization sits on the fence waiting to see if it's "real" or not, and 30 percent resists change. We were aware we would need to face these resistors, but we didn't spend a lot of time on them. We focused instead on championing the change agents to help us drive the new culture.

With the Behavior Outage over, has the work force embraced the culture change?

What you're asking about is momentum. As a management team, we recognize when we're letting the momentum slip, and I'm extremely pleased with our ability to recognize that. The management team owns that and jumps on it right away to make adjustments to keep the energy level up and the changes going. Can I say that we have driven to 100 percent on our change agents? No, but we continue to work hard at driving the highly accountable behaviors throughout all of our supervisors and the entire workforce.

Do you know if any other nuclear plants in the U.S. or internationally have conducted an outage like this?

Not to my knowledge. Certainly, organizations recognize that in order to get good results they need to have good behaviors. However it's difficult to drive those behavior changes throughout an organization.

Did any department at Prairie Island benefit more than others because of the Behavior Outage?

One of the things we're striving for is to break down "department silos" [isolation]. The fact that our managers think first as station managers and then as department managers puts a contrary spin on that question. I'd say the site benefited most by knocking the silos down between departments.

Is this type of outage going to be conducted at other NMC nuclear plants?

It's a matter of timing at each individual site. But the NMC is looking hard at modeling our accountability because we do want to work on accountability across our fleet of plants.

Has Prairie Island become a trendsetter by having a Behavior Outage?

When we return to being an industry leader, I will answer your question.

Example #2: Field Support Team

Synopsis

A Field Operations team for an international oil and gas production company operating in the Gulf of Mexico called and asked me to help them. They were responsible for supporting all the company's offshore oil platforms.

Though team members were competent, they weren't happy. And they were far from productive. Worst of all, two-thirds of the team members were arrogant and overly aggressive.

After identifying team business goals and psychological goals, I guided them toward creating two Work Agreements: a behavioral Agreement to improve trust and a process Agreement to become a self-managing team.

Just one year later, the team had completely turned around.

They had recommitted to their shared goals and were honoring their Work Agreements. As a result, they experienced:

- 78% increase in teammate trust
- 46% increase in mutual team member support
- 61% increase in complying with decisions
- Over $350,000 in savings

For a **more detailed description** of this team's first year with RMT, go to RightMindedTeamwrok.com, search for and read *How to Create Team Working Agreements That Bring People Together.*

First Workshop

I worked with this team for two years. We met every three months for a total of eight workshops. The first workshop was a two-day event; the others were one-day events.

In the first workshop, we created two Agreements.

The team's "relationships Agreement" addressed such things as proper communication, how to behave when a conflict occurs, and a commitment to resolve any unresolved teamwork issues.

The second Agreement addressed team meetings. Since the team had been recently instructed to become self-managing, conducting efficient and effective meetings was a top priority.

Second & Third Workshops

In the next two workshops, the team created a peer-to-peer assessment process. They also made team strategies that aligned with their profit center's strategic goals.

Below are their actual Team Business Plan and Work Agreements. The plan presented here was their second plan, created at the end of their first year.

Additionally, you'll see the results of their Team Performance Assessment Summary, which shows one full year of improvement data.

Large International Oil & Gas Company

Field Support Team's

- Safety & Tactical Plan
- Our Team Business Plan

Who We Are & What We Value

Our goal is to become a high-performing, self-managing team. This Team Business Plan includes the most updated perspectives and strategies for our team.

Who is the "Team?"
Mike: Facilities Representative
Will: Facilities Representative
Mark: Facilities Representative
Sam: Facilities Representative
Bob: Measurement Specialist
Steve: Workover Representative
Steve: Paint / Corrosion Representative

Our Commitment:

As a member of this team, I attest to being an active participant in creating this Team Business Plan and these Work Agreements.

I commit to holding myself accountable and to adhere to them to the best of my ability.

Field Support Team's Business Safety Plan

"Committed to Excellence in Safety"

1. **Full Implementation of STOP Program**
   - A. STOP program to be used on ALL projects supervised. Encourage participation by contractors and operations personnel.
     - a. Route all STOP cards through the MPS who will compile data and forward to E&S Champions for wide distribution of STOP recap report. Track contractor and company participation separately.
     - b. MPS to use the graphical presentation of data for posting as per E&S format.
   - B. Track "Near Misses" through the use of the STOP program.
     - a. E&S Champions to track "Near Misses" on a separate recap report for use at weekly FSG meetings.

2. **Safety Meetings / Information-Sharing**
   - A. Discuss safety issues during weekly FST morning meetings.
     - o Standing agenda items.
       - ▪ Review PDN policies or regulatory updates
       - ▪ Review previous hitch safety-related issues
       - ▪ Review Safety Alerts
     - o Discuss working contractors' recent safety performance & practices to identify potential problems.
     - o List action items.

B. Hold a pre-job meeting with contractor Supervisors and Safety Reps.
   - Perform pre-job walk-through on-location with contract Superintendents, Safety Reps and Company Reps
   - Perform hazards / safety risks assessment.
   - Require ALL contractors to submit JSA before starting work in the field.
   - Review the scope of work and safety guidelines.
   - Hold a post-job meeting with key personnel and share Plus / Delta's with the group.

C. Daily "Operational" Offshore Safety Meeting
   - Conduct meetings in cooperation with the contractor's Foreman / Supervisor / Safety Reps.
   - Identify high potential hazards associated with day's planned activities.
      - Use JSA as a working document for daily safety meetings.
   - Review the previous day's Stop Cards.
   - Include safety meeting topics and discussion in daily construction reports.
   - Maintain a list of attendees. Keep a list in the job file.
   - Perform Level 4 reviews as Standard Operating Procedure. Encourage operations participation.
   - g. Conduct tailgate discussions throughout the day as the scope of work progresses to enhance safety awareness.
   - Document on FST daily safety meeting forms.

D. Utilize E&S Champions.
   - Work closely with E&S to review / critique / develop effective safety meeting agendas.
   - Include E&S Champions in field trips to review job scope with contractors to help in identifying potential safety hazards.
   - Include E&S Champions in ALL accident Root Cause Analysis.
   - Include E&S Champions when possible, to assist in performing top-side surveys to identify safety / compliance-related issues for maintenance work.

3. **Our Team Commitment**
   A. Full support of Team Interaction Agreements for Safety
   - Continue to participate in all team safety training & development workshops.
   - Increase focus on team success in safety.
   - Celebrate our accomplishments and acknowledge our opportunities to improve safety performance as a group.
   - Recognize our diverse workgroup. The team will support individual efforts in safety training and development for the good of the team.

   B. Provide effective communication of safety issues through Team Peer-to-Peer Process.
   - 100% team support of peer-to-peer efforts of honest, open, ongoing communication & feedback to accomplish our safety plan.

4. **Contractor Safety**
   A. Recognize outstanding contractor safety efforts and participation as appropriate.

Team Direction & Strategies

The four strategies listed below are the profit center's strategies. Included are our team's tactics and goals for addressing each strategy.

SS/EI Field Support Strategic Alignment Tactical Plan

Strategy 1 - Aggressively pursue implementation of PP&E

Champions & Responsibilities:
Will & Mark, they will:

- Collect and review all pertinent data every month to make sure the team is on track to accomplish yearly goals.
- Report back to the team.

Tactic 1: Continue to assess risk associated with construction projects through continued implementation of the FST Safety Plan.
Tactic 2: All members are trained in Root Cause Analysis. Perform RCA on near misses, ALL recordable accidents, and spills on construction and maintenance projects. Focus on information-sharing with peers and contractors.
Tactic 3: Continued support of the Contractor Safety Summary / Vendor Retention as a tool in contractor selection. Focus on feedback to E&S and Alliance sponsors on contractor performance.
Tactic 4: Continued use of Self-Review Process performing Level 4 surveys on all construction / maintenance / paint projects. Communicate efforts and results to operations and Facilities Engineers.
Tactic 5: Continue to require 100% reporting of accidents and environmental incidents.

Metrics:

1. Contractor Accident Incident Rate. Goal = IR 3.86
2. # Of Environmental Incidents due to construction. Goal = 2
3. # Of Level 4 Self Reviews performed. Goal = # of AFE projects supervised or greater
4. # Of RCA performed on incidents. Goal = 100% of recordables

Team Agreements

1. Each team member commits to accurate and timely reporting of contractor man-hours; all accidents, types, and number; environmental incidents; level 4 reviews; and all RCA's.

Strategy 2 - Proactively manage our portfolio.

Champions & Responsibilities:
Mike / Steve, they will:

- Track information and report back to the team.
- When the team is not meeting its metrics, the team commits to discuss and agree on how it can get back on track.

Tactic 1: Use surplus equipment and materials as available, utilizing procurement systems in place for determining availability.
Tactic 2: Work closely with FEs to develop AFE project objectives, cost estimates, and tracking processes to effectively meet goals. Examples: pre-job planning, daily cost reporting
Tactic 3: Active support and participation with FMTs in the MOC process.
Tactic 4: Work with Alliance Partners (suppliers) to achieve an inventory of needed stock for delivery in support of AFIS and vendor reduction efforts.

Metrics

1. Shut-in Time (actual vs estimated). Goal = +/- 15% (adjusted for changes in scope of work)
2. AFE costs (actual vs estimated). Goal = +/- 10% (adjusted for changes in scope of work)
3. $ saved by utilization of surplus equipment and materials. Goal = $100M

Team Agreements

1. Each team member will supply champions with needed data, i.e., enough information to justify adjustments for changes in the scope of work.
2. We gladly accept being held accountable for AFEs and downtime we help to plan.

Strategy 3 - Employ Total Quality Management (TQM) to manage our business.

Champions & Responsibilities:
Sam / Bob, they will:

- Announce dates for Alignment sessions and AFIS training.
- Track FST "paid-on-time" invoice statistics.
- Catalog FST Work Process Improvement documentation.

Tactic 1: Identify and prioritize key work processes by discipline, as necessary.
Tactic 2: Flowchart, measure, and improve key work processes that add the highest value to the team (80 / 20).
Tactic 3: Network with Field Support in WCPC to improve info-sharing of best practices and lessons learned.
Tactic 4: Active participation in updates of FST efforts and results at the Strategic Alignment Sessions.

Tactic 5: Support of Alliance Partners with a strong focus on feedback to sponsors in identifying opportunities for improvement.
Tactic 6: Continued consideration of small, disabled, and women-owned / minority businesses in the vendor selection process.
Tactic 7: Support of AFIS accounting system implementation and vendor reduction effort.

Metrics

1. Updates on efforts at Strategic Alignment Sessions. Goal = 3
2. Team participation in AFIS training and usage. Goal = 100%
3. % Of paid-on-time invoices. Goal = 88%
4. # Of key work processes measured and improved. Goal = 2 a year
5. # Of best practices workshops with WCPC field support reps. Goal = semi-annually

Team Agreements

1. Each person will give any work process improvements to champions.
2. Team members will provide evidence of support of the alliance partners and the use of small, disabled, or minority businesses through feedback documentation.

Strategy 4 - Build a committed team and become the "work location of choice."

Champions & Responsibilities:
Mark / Steve, they will:

- Track FST progress toward achieving our metrics and report back to the team.

Tactic 1: Continue informal PMP process as a coaching tool for individual and team performance. Conduct formal individual performance reviews / self-assessments, as necessary.
Tactic 2: Continue to develop and refine the "peer-to-peer" feedback process between team members.
Tactic 3: Continue to practice and refine customer / supplier feedback processes through effective post-job reviews. Focus on improved info-sharing of lessons learned.
Tactic 4: Participate in weekly crew change communication meetings and monthly FE meetings as needed.
Tactic 5: Continue formal team training sessions to improve team interaction and develop new skills.
Tactic 6: 100% commitment and participation by team members in FSG G&A cost-reduction effort. Full support of PC and BU initiatives and info-sharing with peers and O&M to understand and support business drivers guiding cost-reduction efforts.
Tactic 7: Develop consistent guidelines for contractor and company R&A / safety performance recognition to monitor and control costs.

Metrics

1. Team Interaction Questionnaire scores. Goal = 3 times a year
2. # Of post job reviews. Goal = 100% of construction / paint AFEs.
3. Formal Peer-to-Peer team communication exercises. Goal = semi-annually
4. 55% reduction in personal T&E.
5. Monitor cost associated with contractor & company R&A / safety performance recognition awards initiated by FST.
6. Review Team Business Plan semi-annually.

Team Agreements

1. Each team member commits to do their part in completing the above metrics.

Team Performance Factors

As a team, we agreed to evaluate ourselves every quarter and to use these performance factors to keep us on track.

Here are our subjective evaluation criteria:

√ + = we are doing very well
√ = we are doing okay or average
√ - = we need to improve; we're below average
\- = we are not doing this, or we are not doing this very well

Performance Factors [one of their assessments]

1. We are a dynamic team constantly measuring our performance and contributions to the profit center. √
2. We function and interact at such a high level that adjusting our efforts as business needs dictate is an integral part of our process.√

3. As a team, we communicate and function as a "family" on all issues, knowing and trusting that we all have each other's interests in mind. √
4. We recognize and appreciate (value) our differences and similarities and honor our right to be individuals.√
5. We understand, as individuals with our personal preferences and feelings, that personal sacrifice for the good of the team will be a necessary part of our work at certain times. √
6. Our team interaction is at such a high level that sharing responsibility and accountability is never an issue. √–
7. Our personal and professional relationships among team members make recognition and celebration of each other's efforts a naturally occurring part of our team process. –
8. We are a leader in the safety and environmental arena because we adhere to our Field Support Team Safety Plan. √+
9. We have a team culture that is open, honest, and fun. √
10. We optimize available resources for our portfolio management by utilizing surplus equipment, sharing manpower, sharing expertise, etc. √+
11. We meet with customers regularly to discuss expectations, form partnerships, and gain feedback on performance. –
12. Each member knows and accepts their role and responsibilities as they pertain to the team. √
13. We take intelligent risks and explore new opportunities, ideas, and strategies. √
14. We understand our roles and are responsible and accountable for the performance of the profit center. √

Team Processes: Team Meeting Agreements

Agenda Field Support
Tuesday Morning Meeting

6:30 AM to 7:25 AM
Room 3193
Type of meeting
Facilitator:
Note Taker: Crew Change / Information Sharing

Agenda Topics

A. Review Work Agreements for clarity and acknowledgments
B. Technical Information Sharing
C. Activity Recap
D. PP&E - Performance Review
E. Additional Agenda Items:

Team Processes: Peer-to-Peer Process & Agreements

Initially, the Facilities Reps developed the following principles for a Peer-to-Peer Process. Subsequently, the Field Support Team decided to adopt these principles for the entire team as an informal process (meaning no one was to be held accountable for doing these like on their PMP). The team intended to use these principles to improve overall team performance and team member interaction.

Guiding Principles:

1. **Defenselessness communication** - We want to be able to communicate about work situations without getting defensive ... so we can help each other solve / resolve problems. By so doing, we will improve our overall communication ability.
2. **Outside forces will not split us** - Whenever we have outside forces that have the potential to cause us problems (split us), we want to use the Peer-to-Peer Process to help us better understand each other's perspectives and learn how to prevent it next time.
3. **Tom** [their supervisor] **gets a consistent message from us** - We want Tom to get a consistent message from all of us. We also want him to see / believe we're achieving our potential. We intend to improve our working relationship with Tom.
4. "**Who better to talk to**...?" - We want to be able to talk to someone, like each other, who understands what we're up against.
5. **To learn timing and political correctness** - We want to use our discussions to determine on whom, and when, we can push back - like the business team, FMT's, etc. - without causing political and / or PMP problems for ourselves and our customers.
6. **Improve each other's working style** - We want to talk to each other and help each other improve our work styles versus trying to get others to change their style.

7. **Listen -** We want to really listen to each other... which doesn't mean we'll agree, but we won't let any disagreements get in the way of performing our jobs.
8. **Share information -** We intend to share the most appropriate information, realizing that schedules and work objectives get in the way sometimes. For example, it's important for people to attend our Tuesday meetings, but sometimes people can't come.
9. **We will not withhold -** If a teammate hears something about another teammate that's negative (or potentially negative), we'll bring it up to that person and / or the team as soon as appropriate. We intend to help that person and the team.
10. **The Peer-to-Peer is ours -** This process is to be used among ourselves, and it's not for PMP. However, we want it to help us improve in our PMP, avoiding any surprises that Tom might say to us - i.e., "so & so (OS) said ..."
11. **Talk to each other first -** If we have any problem amongst ourselves, we'll discuss it before others find out - especially Tom.
12. **It's an "inside job"** - We want to listen to understand versus listening to respond and judge each other. It's an inside job to notice we're getting defensive or judgmental. We're committed to "STOP" and really listen.
13. **Competitiveness is okay -** We encourage competitiveness, but it's not okay to try to make our light brighter by blowing out someone else's.
14. **We're proud to be a Field Support Team Member** - "I want to stop having to defend myself for being a member of the Field Support Team!"

Team Processes: Relationship Work Agreements

Agreement #1 Intention:

1. Each team member agrees to resolve or help resolve any / all team-related issues.

Conditions for acceptance / clarification:

A. It's our intention to be proactive with each other, to not let any issue go unresolved that would eventually cause problems, and to use this Agreement to improve team performance.

B. Whenever a team member has an issue to resolve, they will first go to others in private, and if they can't resolve it, then they will bring it up to the team.

C. Whenever two or more team members try to resolve an issue, each team member agrees 1) to listen to understand, 2) to swap roles and listen again 3) that no one will get defensive, 4) to express "what's needed," and 5) to resolve.

D. Resolving an issue means each team member will actively support team decisions and accurately represent those decisions to others.

E. We will not use words or body language that make the situation worse.

F. When we see a team member repeatedly breaking this Agreement, and it's a serious breach, we will: 1) address the problem in front of the group, 2) ask them what they feel is the problem, 3) as a group, explain what we feel is the problem, 4) try to resolve the problem, and 5) if we can't resolve, call in a mutually agreed-upon third party.

G. We'll watch our "zingers, joking, and cutting-up" with each other when there's a difficult or tense situation because it only makes things worse and hurts feelings.

H. If something is said and it hurts, "check it out" with them ASAP and resolve it.

I. If a team member needs to vent before they give another team member feedback or to resolve a conflict, it's okay to go to a third party, but it must remain confidential.

Agreement #2 Intention:

2. Each team member commits to support each other.

Conditions for acceptance/clarification:

A. We will review missed opportunities so we will not miss them again.
B. It's our intention to honor our commitment to each other so we can set the "standard" in CPDN.

Agreement #3 Intention:

3. Each team member will work to improve individual and team communications.

Conditions for acceptance/clarification:

A. We will communicate facts and clearly own when what we say could be opinions or assumptions.
B. We will listen to each other's opinions (and repeat it back) to make sure that we really hear each other. We intend to keep an open mind and to change our minds if appropriate.
C. If a team member checks it out with you, it's not about questioning that team member's commitment to the team. We just want to improve our one-on-one team communications.
D. We will not "badmouth" anyone, and we'll be open to feedback if others think we are.
E. When a team member experiences a problem, we'll own it, resolve it, and share the learnings with the team. We will not avoid or deny our role in it.

Team Processes: Team Performance Assessment Summary

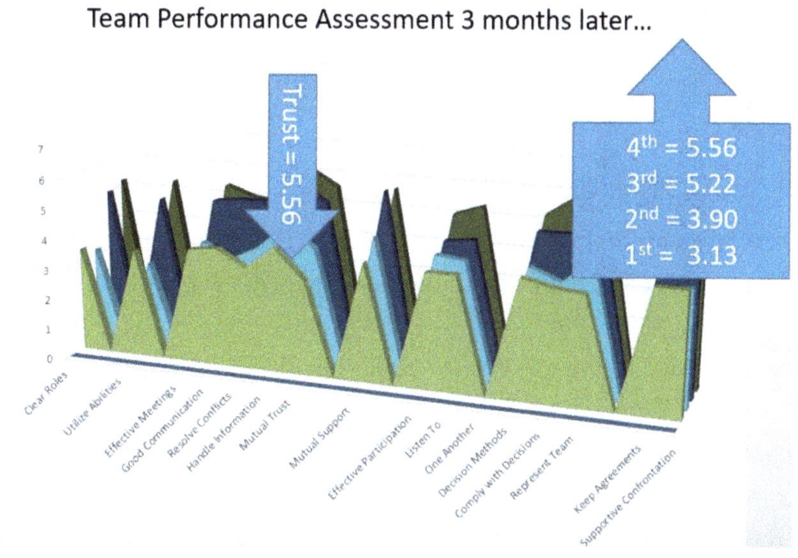

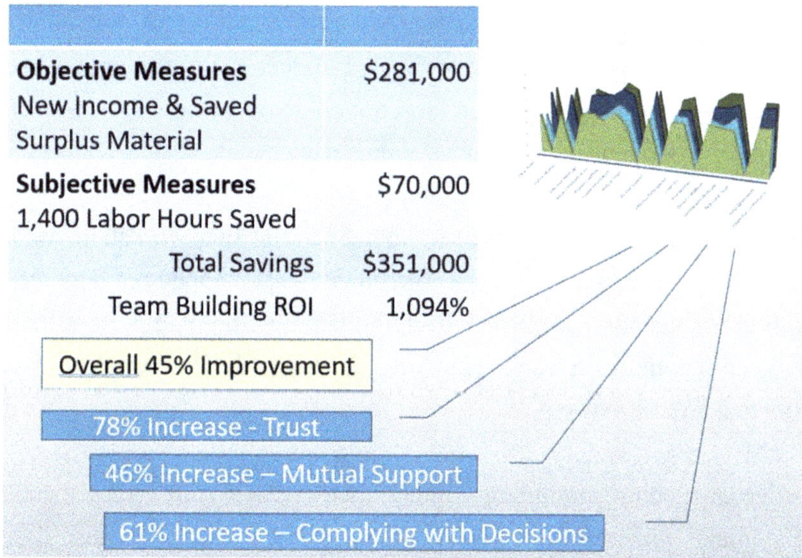

Example #3: International Project Team

Synopsis

Without strong internal processes and teammate trust, teams fall apart.

Such was the experience of Peter and Randy, co-project managers of an 85-person major capital project team. This team was responsible for designing and building a billion-dollar chemical plant.

Twenty-five teammates were from the client organization, which owned the plant. The other teammates were from an international engineering company. All 85 teammates were in the same office.

Team members constantly disagreed over work processes, and toxic interpersonal relationships caused additional stress and dysfunction.

First Workshop

After conducting teammate interviews, I learned many teammates had complaints about the number of required team meetings. They felt meetings were ineffective and not valuable.

We decided this was the issue to address in the first workshop. With support, the team created Work Agreements that mapped out how they would use agendas, identified desired outcomes, and laid ground rules to keep meetings on track. They also addressed how to speak up if a meeting went sideways.

After just one month of living their new Work Agreements, teammates reported they were getting more work done because they were not in so many meetings, and the meetings they did have were more productive, organized, and better facilitated.

The team declared the Work Agreements a success, and managers Randy and Peter estimated **they were able to save $10,000 a week in labor costs.**

Second & Third Workshops

This team wanted to move quickly. They scheduled their second workshop just three weeks after the first. In that workshop, they wanted to address team communications.

And just two weeks after that, they conducted their third workshop, where they addressed prioritizing work.

Here is a summary of their team conclusions. Below, you'll find their Team Business Plan with Work Agreements.

Summary of Team Recommendations

1. Meeting Behaviors: commit to living the Agreement below
2. Type of meeting & frequency changes [see below]
3. PDN: follow agreed upon process [by June 11 training]
4. Weekly reports: change to bi-weekly
5. Make realistic promises between PMT / Client
6. Improve Client Communications: follow agreement below
7. Roles & Responsibilities: clarify as needed
8. QII: First Things First philosophy: commit to live
9. Teammates agree to follow issued plans and procedures.

Teamwork Issue: Meetings

Teammates: Darlene, Troy, Ernest

The Problem is…

a. There are too many valueless and unorganized (impromptu) meetings.
b. Our meetings are not efficient or effective.
c. There is lack of action item tracking and follow-through.
d. There is a lack of consistent meeting notes and no decision register or action item register.

The Opportunity is …

a. To reduce total meeting time and use that extra time toward achieving our schedule.
b. To get more done in the meetings we attend – i.e., become more effective & efficient.
c. To increase our team's performance in completing action items on time.

The Actions recommended are …

1. **Ask all teammates to follow the letter and spirit of our Meeting Process Agreement** (see Agreement in next section)
    a. Steps to endorsement:
        i. Present this Agreement and meeting frequency changes to PMT for feedback, modification, and agreement.
        ii. After PMT and the Advisory team agree, leads will roll out the Agreement to all teammates and ask for their endorsement.

2. **Clarify types of meetings and frequency**.
   a. Summary of "Meeting" Recommendations:
      i. Reduce Morning Meeting to once per week; now called Weekly Meeting
      ii. Add Engineering Leads Meeting – conduct as needed
      iii. Capture Actions in IMS
      iv. BENEFIT: total time save is ~60+ man-hours per week

   b. Weekly Meeting
      i. Frequency & length: Monday, 10–11AM
      ii. Owner: Cary
      iii. Purpose: Ensure all staff are aligned for the week ahead
      iv. Agenda: Cary will publish if deemed necessary
      v. Scribe: Sara / PE will capture action items internal IMS, in real-time
      vi. Attendees: discipline lead, PMT, project engineers

   c. **Engineering "Issues" Meeting** - as-needed meeting
      i. Frequency & Length: this will NOT BE A PANIC MEETING. You will be given no less than 24-hours' notice.
      ii. Purpose: address pressing, and common issues as needed
      iii. Owner: Linda
      iv. Scribe: Troy / other will capture action items internal IMS, in real-time
      v. Attendees: if you are invited
      vi. Agenda: will accompany the notice

d. **PMT - as-needed meeting**

   i. Frequency & length: Every other Thursday 3:00 – 4:00 PM
   ii. Owner: Randy
   iii. Purpose: Discuss and clarify strategic issues such as task / role prioritization over the next 1-3 weeks
   iv. Agenda: Randy will publish if deemed necessary
   v. Scribe: Sara / PE will capture action items internal IMS, in real-time
   vi. Attendees: PMT

e. **PDN / Value Improvement capture**

   i. Frequency & Length: TBD - Tuesday 8:00 – 8:30AM
   ii. Owner: Linda
   iii. Scribe: Sara
   iv. Attendees: Project engineers, discipline leads, PMT
   v. Agenda: review last week's PDN

f. **Value Added Improvement Meeting**

   i. Frequency & length: TBD
   ii. Owner: Randy
   iii. Purpose: show clients how we add value
   iv. Agenda: TBD
   v. Scribe: Sara / PE will capture action items internal IMS, in real-time
   vi. Attendees: PMT

g. Procurement Meeting

i. Frequency & length: TBD
ii. Owner: Cary
iii. Purpose: Ensure orders are placed on time
iv. Agenda: TBD
v. Scribe: Sara / PE will capture action items internal IMS, in real time
vi. Attendees: PMT

h. Schedule Review Meetings

i. Frequency & length: TBD
ii. Owner: Randy
iii. Purpose: Ensure PMT is making progress
iv. Agenda: TBD
v. Scribe: Sara / PE will capture action items internal IMS, in real time
vi. Attendees: PMT

i. External Meetings

i. We recommend IOU teammates use the Meeting Process Agreement in all external meetings.
ii. We recommend that in the near future, when the PMT conducts an integrated team building workshop, the IOU presents this Agreement to the client and asks them if they would be willing to live by these practices.

Meeting Process Agreement

Team Choice:

1. Each teammate will do their part to ensure we have effective and efficient meetings.

Clarifications / Conditions for Acceptance:

A. All regularly scheduled meetings will have a clear purpose, clear outcomes, a realistic agenda distributed 24 hours in advance [identify preparation task], and the right people in attendance.

B. Regularly scheduled meetings will have a meeting owner who is responsible for facilitating and keeping the meeting on track. They will ensure proper meeting notes are taken and distributed.

C. Meeting closure: We will always restate our decision, understanding, and actions-owner-due-by-dates at the end of all meetings.

D. Action Items will be captured in IMS.

E. We agree to use the same level of efficiency and effectiveness in all informal meetings.

F. Everyone will make their thinking visible, even if it means expressing disagreement.

G. Meeting Ground Rules:

- Show up on time, stay on task, and end on time.
- "Let's take it outside." "Enough, let's move on."
- Use the parking lot to capture important but not urgent ideas that will be addressed in future meetings or assigned to teammates to address.
- Respectful and emotionally mature conversation.
- None of us is as smart as all of us.
- Come to a consensus even if you don't get everything you want.
- Hold yourself and others accountable for living this Agreement.

Teamwork Issue: Communications

Teammates: Jackie, Tatiana, Johan, Michael

The Problem is...

a. There is disagreement as to what information needs to be documented and how.
b. The PDN process does not work effectively.
c. Some important information is withheld and / or not properly communicated from PMT to all teammates and vice versa.
d. There is no agreement as to when we need to use verbal or face-to-face communication as opposed to email or IMS.
e. There is a feeling of us versus them between engineering and PMT.
f. There is no agreed-upon way to express disagreement between teammates and leaders.

The Opportunity is...

a. To save time and to satisfy the client with a more effective PDN process.
b. To provide leaders and teammates with the right information at the right time.
c. To increase PMT and engineering collaboration.
d. To reduce misunderstandings and / or increase our likelihood of meeting the schedule because we are communicating properly, in emotionally mature ways.

The Actions recommended are…

1. **Create a behavioral Work Agreement** to address behavioral or interaction issues.
    a. The team will create the first draft (see below) and present it to the PMT for changes and eventual agreement.
    b. The teammates and the PMT leaders will cascade down this Agreement to all IOU teammates

2. **Improve client communication**.
    a. We recommend all teammates use the following "go bys" below to guide our client communications.
    b. We do this because there are times when verbal communication is sufficient and other times when communication needs to be documented.
    c. We recommend that our company provide more or additional training on how to use electronic project communications tools and software.

3. **Update weekly reports**.
    a. To add value and to save time, move to bi-weekly reports that are aligned with or sync with In-Control.

4. **Set realistic promises** between PMT and Client.
    a. Philosophy: Manage and adhere to the Quadrant II / First-Things-First model (see below).
    b. We recommend PMT first discuss deliverable due date promises with discipline leads before making promises to the client.
    c. If our discipline counterpart comes to you with last-minute requests, we will be firm. We can't accept last minute requests all the time. We don't want to accept bad planning on their part.
    d. We recommend all these because:
        i. It will help mitigate us vs. them (engineering vs. PMT).
        ii. It will help mitigate last-minute "drop stuff on my desk" incidents.
    e. We all agreed to the above.

5. **Clarify the IOU PDN process**.
    a. Leaders have discussed and agreed on the internal PDN process. The process will be vetted with the Client and then rolled out to all to follow.

Communications Agreement

Team Choice:
Each team member will communicate their thoughts and feelings in an emotionally mature and professional way.

Clarifications / Conditions for Acceptance:

A. We follow the spirit & intent of our One Way Values.
B. Emotional and professional mature communication can be described as tone of voice, word choice, body language, assertive versus aggressive, etc.
C. When we notice disagreement or tension in a conversation, we will stop and define terms or facts. We also commit to using the What to Say statements.
D. If we feel or believe another is being inappropriate, we will remind them of this Communications Agreement.
E. We also agree to give positive reinforcement to our teammates when we see or hear effective communication.
F. Not only do we agree to hold ourselves accountable, but we will also hold others accountable in a safe and supportive way, and that means we will speak up and not keep silent.
G. We don't condone behind-the-back negative conversation. We advocate that all teammates discuss their frustrations and resolve them.
H. If a team member continues to break any of our team Work Agreements, we will escalate this issue to a higher authority.

What to Say

Use these statements to advocate, inquire, or resolve conflict on any team.

Improved Advocacy

- Here's what I'm thinking and how I got there…
- Some of the assumptions I've made are…..

Improved Inquiry

- What data are you using to reach that conclusion…?
- What's leading you to make that conclusion…?

When You Disagree

- Tell me again how you came to believe this point of view.
- Are you using any data that I may not have considered?
- Am I understanding you correctly that you're saying…?

Dealing with an Impasse

- What do we know for a fact?
    - What do we think is true but don't have any data for yet?
    - Are there things we don't know?
    - What is unknowable?
- It seems / feels like we're at an impasse. Do you have ideas that might help us come to a new Work Agreement?

Teamwork Issue: Prioritize Work, Tasks, Packages
Teammates: Sumiti, Lora, Linda, Sharon

The Problem is…

a. There are too many last-minute requests that cause panic.
b. There are too many unrealistic requests / deadlines.
c. Too often teammates are not aware of and / or don't follow established procedures.

The Opportunity is…

a. To save time by reducing last-minute crisis situations and by being more flexible.
b. To increase our internal collaboration, plus our collaboration with our customers.
c. To create alignment between all IOU teammates and leaders as to what is realistic.

Statements of Fact…

a. When the Service Order is signed, and the schedule is published, prioritization will help.
b. Until the reorganization and alignments are published, there will be uncertainty in people's minds as to our priorities.
c. We believe that living the other sub-team Agreements will help resolve the "prioritization" issue.

The Actions recommended are…

1. **Adopt / agree to live by First-Things-First.**
    a. Ask all PMT leaders and leads to abide by the QII First-Things-First philosophy (see next section) and adopt it as an individual responsibility.

2. **Ask teammates to do the following.**
    a. If you believe you and your direct project supervisor are not aligned with respect to your work task prioritization, stop immediately to talk about it and resolve it.
    b. If you are asked by your direct project supervisor to stop what you are doing and do something else, seek to understand why. Maybe it is not really a crisis. However, if you go forward with the new task, be certain to negotiate and agree on what you will and will not do.

3. **Ask all teammates to follow the issued plans and procedures.**
    a. When gaps or misunderstandings are discovered, use accepted Client and Engineering Company procedures.

First Things First: A Time Management Philosophy

	Urgent	Not Urgent
Important	QI: Crisis, panic, pressing problems, missed deadlines, "fires" you have to address now	**QII:** Proper / realistic planning, crisis prevention, building positive relationships, having enough time to complete deliverables **Say YES!**
Not Important	QIII: Interruptions: hallway talk, last-minute requests for info Say No...	QIV: Low value or duplicate work Say No...
	Time	

Teamwork Issue: Roles & Responsibilities

Teammates: Sara, Carlos, Guillermo

The Problem is…

a. There is a misalignment of roles and responsibilities in some areas.
b. There is confusion and lack of understanding of PMT roles and responsibilities.
c. Too often teammates don't feel empowered or engaged.
d. There is a feeling of us versus them between engineering and PMT.

The Opportunity is…

a. To improve effectiveness and efficiency by having a greater number of teammates and leaders aligned on roles and responsibilities.
b. To increase the likelihood of meeting the schedule because a greater number of teammates and leaders are following through on their roles and responsibilities.
c. To increase PMT and engineering collaboration.
d. To increase trust, accountability, and collaboration throughout the project team.

Statements of Fact…

a. We believe that living the other sub-team Agreements will help resolve the "prioritization" issue.

The Actions recommended are…

1. Realize we are currently in a re-alignment with our client.
    a. Some of the role ambiguity could be mitigated in the new alignment.

2. Empower individual teammates through growth.
    a. Growing individual capability is important. Therefore, we recommend PMT, and department leads do more to empower individual teammates to help them grow and develop.

3. Speak up if not in agreement.
    a. If any teammate or leader believes they are not in agreement with respect to their roles, responsibility, and duties, they have PMT's permission to speak to their direct supervisor.
    b. Follow these steps:
        i. Review your roles as listed in the PEP.
        ii. Identify any changes you'd like to make such as where you believe you should have more empowerment.
        iii. Discuss with your direct project supervisor.
        iv. Come to an agreement.
        v. If you can't come to an agreement, team leaders will make the decision.

4. Optional: Clarify roles through group activity.
    a. If deemed of value, use the following roles exercise.
    b. Consider a lunch-and-learn where all key roles are presented and clarified.

Roles & Responsibilities Team-Building Workshop Agenda

Desired Outcome: Discuss, clarify, confirm, and agree on who does what, when, and how.

Time Commitment: 2-4 hours
Participants: 7 teammates

Agenda

A. Kick-off
B. Agree on the Desired Outcome
C. Agree to believe and behave as one unified team
D. RMT's Role Clarification exercise
    - One person at a time gives answers to the questions.
    - Dialogue follows.
    - Time permitting, create new Work Agreements & teammate understandings
    - Capture conclusions in the Team Business Plan.
    - If you run out of time, complete as many possible, then schedule a second session to continue.
E. Close

Example #4: Architectural Design Company

Synopsis

This is the story of an architectural design firm with over 100 employees. Leroy, the partner-in-charge, asked, "Can you facilitate one of those off-site meetings you do?"

I told him I'd be happy to. "What do you want to accomplish?" I asked.

He said he wanted to increase trust and to get the other founding partner to change his work behavior. The partner was driving everyone crazy. He was making customers angry. He was even running off some of their best employees.

My prospective client wanted his partner to stop all the whining and complaining. The company was having its best year ever, and he didn't want to blow it!

After I interviewed all the other partners and principles, I validated the head partner's perception. There was a lack of trust. The other leaders were also very frustrated with the other founding partner. Most believed that if he were gone, their problems would be solved.

I learned in the interviews that the organization had very little team and organizational structure. They had no strategic plan and no team operating system. Everyone agreed they needed a vision and more structure.

I reported back to the head partner and reflected on what I was seeing.

I said, "Sometimes, the best way to address dysfunctional behavior is first to resolve work process issues. I recommend that in the offsite meeting, we create the organization's first strategic plan and operating structure. Once that is in place if a particular leader or partner doesn't do their part, then you can easily implement corrective action or termination."

He agreed to that plan.

First Workshop

In the first workshop, the team created five strategies, along with several process and behavioral Work Agreements. They even took the time to clarify roles and responsibilities.

They also agreed I would facilitate their leadership team meetings as part of the improvement process.

Second & Third Workshop

In place of additional formalized workshops, I facilitated the team's biweekly leadership team meetings for the next six months.

During our time together, we made our way through every one of Right-Minded Teamwork's 5 Elements. Below is their Team Business Plan.

***Note**: This final example has been abbreviated down to the essentials since there are already two preceding Team Business Plan examples, which include full details.*

ABC Architectural Design Firm

Mission Statement

To provide quality architecture through personal service that responds to our clients' needs while providing a vibrant, positive environment for our employees.

Summary of Strategic Goals

Strategic Goal 1:
Deliver Exceptional Architectural Design & Service (details below)

Strategic Goal 2:
Be an Awesome Place to Work (details below)

Strategic Goal 3:
Increase the Financial Value of Firm

Strategic Goal 4:
Expand Present Markets & Capture New Ones

Strategic Goal 5:
Contribute to Our Community

Strategic Goals

Strategic Goal 1: Deliver Exceptional Architectural Design & Service

Sponsor: Marc

Important Perspectives:

- Clients & prospective clients
- Suppliers / JVs / Contractors
- Community – a sense of pride in ABC's work
- ABC's employees – a sense of pride

Focus:

- Quality, innovation, TQM service to clients
- Creating a learning organization
- Vertical Studio work-process efficiency
- Efficient, competent, talented, and productive employees

ACTIONS

1.1: Create, implement, and follow an Exceptional Design Standard that will ensure we raise the bar on the level of our design.

a. Describe & define the "exceptional" service standard.
b. Train employees in 1) the ABC Exceptional Service Standard, and 2) capture specific service standards for each employee in their individual performance plans.
c. Create and implement a client satisfaction "exceptional service" scorecard process to understand how ABC is doing and identify needed areas for improvement.

1.2 Maintain a continuous-improvement, total-quality process in all phases and levels at ABC.

Proposal & Contract Stage

a. Improve the entire proposal-to-contract process so both clients and ABC employees have a positive experience while creating clear deliverables, timelines, accountabilities, and other quality and service expectations.

Presentation Stage

a. Improve ABC's marketing presentation capability.

Job Stage

a. Fully implement the Vertical Team process.
b. Fully implement the QA / QC process.
c. Implement a web-based project management site for design and construction.

Follow-up Stage

a. Consistently follow-up on projects.

Strategic Goal 2: Be an Awesome Place to Work
Sponsor: Bob

Important Perspectives:

- Employees
- ABC management
- Clients / Suppliers / Industry

Focus:

- Just and fair rewards, benefits, and compensation
- Retention / turnover / recruitment
- Happy / satisfied employees
- The right people, with the right skills, in the right jobs, at the right time

ACTIONS

2.1: Ensure the right people with the right skills are in the right job at the right time and are delivering "exceptional architectural service."

a. Create an awesome, effective, unified leadership team that is fun to work with.
b. Establish and implement a partner peer review system using a Leadership 360 upward appraisal system.
c. Agree on Associate's roles, and accountabilities.

2.2: Create an awesome, can-do, positive ABC culture and physical environment.

a. Create and implement an annual, confidential employee perception survey (conduct two surveys in the first 12 months, then annually thereafter).
b. Ensure the Employee Performance Review system is indeed helping the firm 1) have the right people with the right skills and 2) meet or exceed ABC's five Strategic Goals.

2.3: Develop and implement a standardized, flexible interviewing / hiring process using behavioral-based concepts, candidate accomplishments, and ABC's Strategic Goals.

a. Develop minimum competency hiring standards for key positions.

2.4: Develop a leadership / employee training and development strategy that directly links to ABC's five Strategic Goals.

a. Leadership: Using the leader upward appraisal / individual improvement plan, the firm will support / fund the leader to attend training to improve leadership skills.
b. Employee: Using the individual performance reviews and the (potential) employee survey to identify needed training, the firm will support / fund training and development courses for employees.
c. Improve communication of office procedures, standards, and policies.

2.5: Ensure ABC has a just and fair rewards and compensation system.

a. Assess the current formal and informal compensation system that will help ABC meet or exceed its Strategic Goals.

2.6: Celebrate our company, team, and individual successes.

a. Create ways to celebrate with our clients, suppliers, and employees.

Sample Roles & Responsibilities

Example 1: Leroy

What do I contribute to the firm?

- Leadership through final decision-making when required to resolve issues
- Personal and professional presence in the community through volunteer organizations and political activities
- Primary networking, public relations, and project procurement effort
- Provide the glue to hold the organization stable

What authority do I currently have?

- President and chairman of the board of directors
- Own majority of voting stock
- Can make final decisions (only with the majority of board vote)

What do I need?

- Need no further authority and feel no boundaries within the framework of what we all agree to as the best interest of the firm

Leroy: What Will I…

START

1. Be more organized: delegate direct project-related issues, solicit feedback regularly from principals, receive feedback from principals regarding when I am being impulsive
2. Push/direct people back to solving own interpersonal relationships
3. Spend more time with employees, getting to know them – dedicating the time to personally interact and recognize contributors
4. Trust all principals in their judgment and level of interest – demonstrate support when delegating, self-monitor behaviors when delegating, forgive the failures, negotiate timelines and expectations, receive, and listen and positively respond to push back from Principals.
5. Share more of the public image of the firm – communicate when events "expect" attendance and when they "may" attend – ask for what is needed, and discuss with Mark to determine in Monday management meeting; ask people to go to events "with me"
6. Be more patient with employees and Principals – ask for feedback and coaching; increase self-awareness of body language and tone of voice
7. Recognize that everyone doesn't think and make decisions like me – raise self-awareness, self-monitor reactions to different styles, rely on trust

STOP

1. Being stressed out by daily situations – focus on the "start," delegate project-specific issues, personally commit to making the mental shift; double-check when delegating actions
2. Being impatient – (see above)
3. Working 12-hour days – schedule a vacation; make the mental shift that it won't end if I give responsibility away
4. Letting the activities and demands of our clients control my life – reprioritize events and communicate priorities to peers

CONTINUE

1. To provide leadership and vision for the firm
2. Mentor those I feel have the ability and drive to succeed
3. Make the firm financially successful by obtaining high-profit projects
4. Take the image of the firm to the highest level possible
5. Follow my plan to dispose of my stock in the firm and retire

Example 2: Bob

What do I contribute to the firm?

- A liaison in computer technology between users and non-users of CAD (because I took it upon myself to understand the system and its implications)
- Heavily involved in staffing human resource functions
- Agent of change for policies that beg to be implemented because they have been successfully used by other companies whose growth rates have similarly demanded change
- The implementer of solutions that are necessary to achieve the goals and vision of the company
- Represent this firm as one of its leaders

What authority do I currently have?

- Review and make recommendations for software and equipment purchases related to CAD
- Suggest alternatives in our policies and decisions
- PIC lead committee member for human resources
- Draft proposals for projects and give input to others when asked

What do I need?

- Receive input and increase staff before a crisis occurs
- Change the culture in ways beneficial to the firm
- Support of all other Principles in enhancing our image through understanding and dedication to quality programs and policies

ABC Architectural Design Process Work Agreements

1. Each Principal will either print their own budget reports OR provide a list of job numbers to their accounting contact person to get the budget reports.
    - Schedule time with the Project Manager to discuss budget and completion reports.
    - Create a plan of action; ensure that the Project Manager understands where they are on the project and what needs to happen to ensure a quality project is delivered within budget and on time.
    - PIC meets with PMs twice per month.

2. "Design people" (Leroy, Mark, Marc, Cheryl) will meet together to decide what to do with controversial designs during the proposal phase.
    - What can we do within the budget?
    - How much are we willing to invest of ABC's money?
    - Do we go back to the client & sell the design to get more money?
    - If it is determined that the project will require an ABC investment, present to Management Team for: Approval Veto, Alternative solutions

The team also made two additional process Agreements two weeks later:

3. Print and establish a list of PIC, PM to input into the Win2 system.
    a. Ensure Ralph checks the list for accuracy.

4. We agree that if we cannot accomplish the outcomes & accountabilities, we agreed to, we will raise the issue with Principles to re-evaluate & prioritize

And, after another four weeks, the team added another three process Agreements:

5. Discuss Aged Receivables at the last Management Meeting each month.
    a. Accounting to provide Aged Receivables to Stephanie by Wednesday prior to distribution and review.
    b. Each Principal agrees to review the Aged Receivables Report prior to the Management Meeting.
6. A report will not be labeled "final" until an assessment of the accounting system has been made and agreement by Management Team has been reached regarding how the "profitability" of a project is reported.

7. Every two weeks in our Management Meeting, we will discuss Forecast Staffing Needs (at the end of the meeting).
    a. We agree that Ralph should be present for this portion of the meeting.
    b. Leroy should share any relevant information early on and is excused from this portion of the meeting.

Architectural Design Action Work Agreements

Intention:

1. When we discuss and agree on our individual roles and responsibilities, we will be open and honest (in a business context); we will address the issue and not attack the person.

Conditions for Acceptance / Clarifications:

- None were made for this Agreement.

Intention:

2. Each team member agrees to address issues without getting defensive.

Conditions for Acceptance / Clarifications:

A. If someone does get defensive, it's okay if we acknowledge it, quickly apologize for it, and move on.
B. It's not about being perfect. It's about recovery and rebounding.
C. If someone does get defensive, we will:
    - Reframe the issue
    - Ask, "Are you feeling defensive…?"
    - Say, "I'm sorry, but I don't think you understand my point…will you reflect back to me what you're hearing me say?"

Intention:

3. We will discuss and agree to upfront on the ABC direction we are going, and we will all visibly support that decision.

Conditions for Acceptance / Clarifications:

A. If we feel a Principal has not upheld this Agreement, we will bring it up with that Principal and remind them of this Agreement. We will provide behavior-specific and / or specific examples of instances when we perceived this Agreement was not being upheld. We will resolve the issue.

B. Our intention for this Agreement is to be unified outside this room, and when we have disunity, we work it out in this room.

Intention:

4. We will address each other one-on-one when there is a difficult issue with the intent to resolve and reach an agreement.

Conditions for Acceptance / Clarifications:

A. If we cannot reach an agreement, we will raise difficult issues in a group setting with the intent to reach an agreement. We will not engage inside conversations with the intent of avoiding or politicking.

Intention:

5. If a Principal feels that they are overloaded and cannot perform all the tasks or meet all the expectations, they will call it out at the Management Meeting.

Conditions for Acceptance / Clarifications:

A. If we perceive a Principal is overloaded and is not meeting expectations, we will call it out.
B. Our intention for this Agreement is to create the right work workload balance to meet our Strategic Plan.
C. Whenever possible, we will educate / inform each other on our current workload (increase understanding of what is on each other's plate) so that we improve our work efficiencies, like reducing callbacks.

Intention:

6. We will not engage in negative discussions about another Principal.

Conditions for Acceptance / Clarifications:

A. If a Principal speaks negatively about another, we will stop them and encourage them to work that issue out with that Principal.
B. We will provide assistance and guidance in helping each other go back to the source and reach an agreement.

The End

On behalf of **Reason** and all the **Right-Minded Teammate Decision-Makers**, we extend our best wishes to you and your teammates as you create another ***Right-Minded Team that Works Together as One***.

www.ingramcontent.com/pod-product-compliance
Lightning Source LLC
Chambersburg PA
CBHW061207220326
41597CB00015BA/1546
* 9 7 8 1 9 3 9 5 8 5 0 5 9 *